I0113483

The Gaming Addiction Workbook

Information, Assessments, and Tools for Managing Life with a Behavioral Addiction

Ester R.A. Leutenberg and John J. Liptak, EdD

Whole Person Associates

101 West 2nd Street, Suite 203
Duluth, MN 55802-5004

800-247-6789

Books@WholePerson.com
WholePerson.com

The Gaming Addiction Workbook

Printed in the United States of America

Editorial Director: Jack Kosmach
Art Director: Mathew Pawlak
Cover Design: Adam Sippola
Editor: Peg Johnson

Library of Congress Control Number: 2020943219
ISBN:978-1-57025-363-8

From the co-authors, Ester and John
Our gratitude, thanks, and appreciation
to the following professionals:

Editorial Directors – Jack Kosmach & Peg Johnson

Editor and Life-long Teacher – Eileen Regen, MEd, CIE

Reviewers – Niki Tilicki, MA Ed & Eileen Jonatis, MA Ed

Proof-reader and Reviewer – Jay Leutenberg, CASA

Art Director – Mathew Pawlak

A Special Thank You
to
Whole Person Associates

for their interest in mental health issues.

Free PDF Download Available

To access your free PDF download of the assessment tools
and all of the reproducible activities in this workbook, go to:
https://WholePerson.com/store/TheGamingAddictionWorkbook3219.html

Understanding Behavioral Addictions

There are many types of addictions. The addictions that have been talked about most have been substance abuse addictions. However, behavioral addictions can occur that take the same form as a physical dependence on substances.

> It is the compulsive nature of the behavior that is often indicative of a behavioral addiction, or process addiction, in an individual. The compulsion to continually engage in an activity or behavior despite the negative impact on the person's ability to remain mentally and/or physically healthy and functional in the home and community defines behavioral addiction. The person may find the behavior rewarding psychologically or get a "high" while engaged in the activity but may later feel guilt, remorse, or even overwhelmed by the consequences of that continued choice. Unfortunately, as is common for all who struggle with addiction, people living with behavioral addictions are unable to stop engaging in the behavior for any length of time without treatment and intervention.
>
> ~American Addiction Centers

People are increasingly experiencing non-substance behavioral addictions, and diminished control over the behavior. No longer categorized as impulse disorders, behavioral addictions are now being viewed as true addictions, much like substance abuse.

The National Institute of Health (2010) states:

> Growing evidence suggests that behavioral addictions resemble substance addictions in many domains, including natural history, phenomenology, tolerance, comorbidity, overlapping genetic contribution, neurobiological mechanisms, and response to treatment.

The concept of addiction, for years used to indicate the use of psychotropic substances, is now being applied to describe a heterogeneous group of syndromes known as "behavioral addictions," "no-drug addictions," or "new addictions." Prevalence rates for such conditions are amongst the highest registered for mental disorders with social, cultural, and economic implications. Individual forms of behavioral addictions are linked by a series of psychopathological features that include repetitive, persistent, and dysfunctional behaviors, loss of control over behavior in spite of the negative repercussions of the latter, compulsion to satisfy the need to implement the behavior, initial well-being produced by the behavior, craving, onset of tolerance, abstinence, and, ultimately, a progressive, significant impairment of overall individual functioning.

Why Are They Called Behavioral Addictions?

Behavioral addictions constitute any maladaptive pattern of excessive behavior that manifests in physiological, psychological, and cognitive symptoms such those listed below.

- **Continuance:** Continuation of the behavior despite knowing that this activity is creating or exacerbating physical, psychological and/or interpersonal problems.

- **Intention effects:** Inability to stick to one's routine, as evidenced by exceeding the amount of time devoted to the behavior or consistently going beyond the intended amount.

- **Lack of control:** Unsuccessful attempts to reduce the level of the behavior or cease it for a certain period of time.

- **Reduction in regular daily activities:** Social, familial, occupational, and/or recreational activities occur less often or are stopped as a direct result of the behavior.

- **Time:** Excessive time is spent preparing for, engaging in, and recovering from the behavior.

- **Tolerance:** Increase in the extent of the behavior in order to feel the desired effect, a "buzz", or a sense of accomplishment.

- **Withdrawal:** Anxiety, irritability, restlessness, and sleep problems affect the person in the absence of the addictive behavior.

Video Game Addictions?

Video game addictions, also known as gaming disorders, or internet gaming disorders, are generally defined as a problematic, compulsive use of video and/or internet games that results in significant impairment to a person's ability to function in various life domains over a prolonged period of time. The American Medical Association (2007) defines heavy game use as playing video games for more than two hours per day. Estimates of the amount of time gamers spend playing video games vary from 6 to 12 hours per week. Some reports suggest that gamers actually spend about a quarter of their leisure time playing video games.

As with all types of behavioral and physical addictions, the possibility of a video game addiction is not only the amount of time spent gaming, but also the function it is serving for the individual. Video game playing, like other recreational activities, may not be harmful or indicate an addiction. However, when game playing becomes addictive, it can take over as the person's main way of coping with life, with other important areas of life being neglected or disrupted as a result.

Gaming Disorder in the DSM-5

The World Health Organization (2018) added "gaming disorder" to the 2018 version of its medical reference book, International Classification of Diseases. It recognizes "Gaming Disorder" in their International Classification of Diseases (ICD-11) as:

A pattern of persistent or recurrent gaming behavior, which may be online or offline, manifested by impaired control over gaming, increasing priority given to gaming to the extent that gaming takes precedence over other life interests and daily activities, and continuation or escalation of gaming despite the occurrence of negative consequences.

While the American Psychiatric Association (2018) does not recognize video game addiction as a disorder, they included video game addiction as a "condition requiring further study" in the Diagnostic and Statistical Manual of Mental Disorders. Video game addiction is a broader concept than internet gaming addiction, but most video game addiction is associated with internet gaming. APA suggests the symptoms and effects of video game addiction are similar to those of other proposed behavioral addictions. Video game addiction may be an impulse control disorder, similar to compulsive gambling.

The APA explains why Internet Gaming Disorder has been proposed as a disorder: The American Psychiatric Association published the fifth edition of its Diagnostic and Statistical Manual of Mental Disorders, commonly referred to as the DSM-5. As of 2019, although Gaming Disorder has not been officially included, the DSM-5 does include a section to help people and doctors know the warning signs of problem video gaming. These problems can occur whether one plays online or offline. According to criteria that were proposed in the DSM-5 one needs to have five or more of these signs in one year to consider it to be a problem. Below are actions to notice:

- Avoiding or closing out social relationships.
- Feeling bad when they cannot play.
- Having problems at work, school, or home because of gaming.
- Lying to people close to them about how much time they spend playing.
- Needing to spend more and more time playing to feel good.
- Not being able to quit or even play less.
- Not wanting to do other activities that they used to like.
- Playing despite these problems.
- Thinking about gaming all or a lot of the time.
- Using gaming to ease bad moods and feelings.

Additional Warning Signs of Video Game Addiction

It can be difficult to notice the difference between enjoying playing video games and a full-blown addiction to playing video games.

Here are some of the warning signs of video game addiction.

- A decrease in personal hygiene or grooming.
- Declining life achievement.
- Dropping out of usual activities.
- Feeling restless, moody, depressed, or irritable when attempting to cut down on the use of video games.
- Gaming for longer periods of time than originally intended.
- Headaches or eye strain from extended playing.
- Inability to set limits on how much time is spent gaming.
- Inability to think about almost anything other than constant thoughts about previous on-line activity or anticipation of the next on-line session.
- Irritable, anxious, frustrated, or angry when forced to stop gaming, even for brief periods of time.
- Isolating from family and friends to develop online friends.
- Jeopardizing or risking loss of significant relationships, job, education endeavors, or career opportunities because of game play.
- Lack of face-to-face social relationships.
- Lying to family members, friends, therapists, and others to conceal the extent of involvement in gaming.
- Needing to spend more time playing games or to play more intensely in order to get the same level of enjoyment.
- Neglect of other hobbies or friendships.
- Poor performance at work or household responsibilities as a result of a preoccupation with gaming.
- Repeated, unsuccessful efforts to control, cut back, or stop playing video games.
- Symptoms of physical or psychological withdrawal, such as loss of appetite, sleeplessness, agitation, or emotional outbursts if unable to game.
- Unable to complete tasks and assignments as promised.
- Unusual fatigue, tendency to fall asleep during work.
- Use of video games in increasing amounts of time in order to achieve satisfaction.
- Using gaming to escape from problems or to relieve feelings of hopelessness, guilt, anxiety, and/or depression.
- Using video games as a way to escape stressful situations at school, work, or conflicts at home.

People with a mild video game addiction may exhibit between four and five of these behaviors, while those with a moderately severe video game addiction may exhibit six to seven of these behaviors. People who suffer from a severe video addiction will usually exhibit most all of the behaviors.

Positive Characteristics of Playing Video Games

Although some people view playing video games as strictly a negative activity that will lead to an addiction to video games, there are many ways that video games can actually be positive and provide a wide variety of healthy life skills. Playing video games in a regulated way that does not interfere with daily activities, health, work, school, family life, and relationships can provide some of these positive characteristics.

They can ...

- Acquire greater motor skills.
- Analyze situations quickly.
- Build the ability to execute planned strategies.
- Connect with new people.
- Create problem-solving techniques.
- Decrease stress.
- Define logistics.
- Determine many ways to track many shifting variables.
- Develop a sharpened hand-eye coordination.
- Enhance heightened concentration.
- Establish awareness of how to explore and rethink goals.
- Exercise indoors or outdoors.
- Expand planning strategies.
- Find new skills to be able to respond to frustrations.
- Fine-tune critical-thinking capabilities.
- Fortify motivation to work toward goals.
- Generate skills of multiple objectives.
- Improve decision-making skills.
- Increase capability of overcoming obstacles.
- Learn from mistakes.
- Magnify team work collaboration.
- Practice responses to challenges.
- Refine resource management skills.
- Strengthen capacity to set goals.
- Understand different methods of conflict resolution.

This is not intended to be an exhaustive list of the positive characteristics of playing video games. It is important to acknowledge to participants that these are skills that can be learned when gaming; however it is also important to have a healthy balance between playing video games and living the fullness of one's life successfully.

Types of Video Games

A video game genre is a specific category of games related by similar game play characteristics. Video game genres are not usually defined by the setting or story of the game or its medium of play, but by the way the player interacts with the game. As time goes on, there will be more added to this list.

Action
- Battle Royale
- Beat 'em up games
- Fighting games
- Platform games
- Rhythm games
- Shooter games
- Stealth game
- Survival games

Action-Adventure
- Metroidvania
- Survival horror

Adventure
- Graphic adventures
- Interactive movie
- Real-time 3D adventures
- Text adventures
- Visual novels

Role-Playing
- Action RPG
- First-person party-based RPG
- MMORPG
- Roguelikes
- Sandbox RPG
- Tactical RPG

Simulation
- Construction and management simulation
- Life simulation
- Vehicle simulation

Strategy
- 4X game
- Artillery game
- Auto battler (auto chess)
- Grand strategy wargame
- Multiplayer online battle arena (MOBA)
- Real-time strategy (RTS)
- Real-time tactics (RTT)
- Tower defense
- Turn-based strategy (TBS)
- Turn-based tactics (TBT)
- Wargame

Sports
- Competitive
- Racing
- Sports game
- Sports-based fighting

Other notable genres
- Advergame
- Art game
- Board game or card game
- Casual games
- Idle gaming
- Logic game
- MMO
- Mobile game
- Party game
- Programming game
- Trivia game

Negative Characteristics of Playing Video Games

Studies indicate that playing video games for extended periods of time can negatively affect the brain, memory, and vision. An addiction to video-game play can cause stress, anxiety, and even isolation if the addiction becomes severe enough. Video games can kill brain cells and interrupt a person's sleep.

The following are some of the negative effects of a video game addiction.

Lifestyle Interruption

Gaming addictions result in personal, family, academic, financial, and occupational problems that greatly interrupt life.

Relationship Problems

Real-life relationships are often disrupted as a result of excessive gaming. The people who have a video game addiction are likely to spend more time in lonely seclusion and spend less time with the important people in their lives. They are often viewed as socially awkward. Arguments often result due to the amount of time spent playing and a lack of time spent interacting face-to-face. Video game players may attempt to conceal the amount of time spent playing, which results in distrust and the disturbance of the quality present in once stable relationships.

Financial Consequences

Gaming can become very costly and result in financial consequences. Much of the equipment needed to play video games designed for prolonged use can be quite costly to purchase, and some charge monthly subscription fees as well.

Low Self-Esteem

Some individuals may create on-line personas or "avatars" to alter their identity and pretend to be someone other than who they really are. Those at highest risk for creation of a secret life are those who have low-self-esteem, feelings of inadequacy, and fear of disapproval from others. Such negative self-concepts often lead to problems such as depression and anxiety.

Physical or Medical Problems

Being addicted to video-gaming can cause physical or medical problems such as: carpal tunnel syndrome, dry eyes, backaches, severe headaches, eating irregularities, failure to attend to personal hygiene, and sleep disturbances.

Fantasy Life

People addicted to video games tend to be lonely and socially marginalized. They may have difficulty with real-life social interactions and can develop a social phobia. They may feel that they have a more positive social experience and more control in virtual relationships than they do in real life.

Withdrawal Symptoms

People who attempt to quit video gaming play experience withdrawal symptoms like anger, depression, mood swings, fantasies, anxiety, fear, irritability, sadness, loneliness, boredom, restlessness, procrastination, and physical health issues. Although mental and emotional withdrawal symptoms may be intense, they are a necessary aspect of the recovery process. Withdrawal is different for every person, however, but most people will exhibit some of the symptoms identified above.

Using This Workbook

The purpose of *The Gaming Addiction Workbook* is to provide helping professionals with cognitive and behavioral assessments, tools, and exercises that can be utilized to treat the root psychological causes of a gaming addiction. It is designed to help people identify and change negative, unhealthy thoughts and behaviors that may have led to a gaming addiction. The activities contained in this workbook can help participants identify their triggers that can lead to a preoccupation with playing video games and teach them ways to overcome and manage those triggers.

The Gaming Addiction Workbook will help participants to ...

- Build self-esteem in positive capabilities outside of playing video games.
- Develop greater self-acceptance and the ability to change ineffective behaviors.
- Learn ways to live a new life without a preoccupation with video games.
- Recognize that they are experiencing an addiction problem.
- Reflect and become aware of the behaviors that were part of and arose from the addiction.
- Understand the triggers for preoccupation with video games.
- Understand recurring patterns that indicate a gaming addiction.

The Gaming Addiction Workbook is a practical tool for any professional who works with people living with behavioral addictions. Depending on the role of the person using this workbook and the specific group or individual's needs, the modules can be used either individually or as part of an integrated curriculum. The facilitator may choose to administer one of the activities to a group or use some of the assessments over one or more days as a workshop.

Confidentiality When Completing Activity Handouts

Participants will see the words **"NAME CODES"** on some of the activities in the modules. Instruct participants that when writing or speaking about anyone, they should use name codes for people to preserve privacy and anonymity. This will allow participants to explore their feelings without hurting anyone's feelings or fearing gossip, harm or retribution. For example, a friend named Shana who **R**ides **A M**otorcycle might be assigned a name code of **R.A.M.** for a particular exercise. In order to protect others' identities, they should not use people's actual names or initials, just NAME CODES.

The Five Modules

This workbook contains five separate modules of activity-based handouts that will help participants learn more about themselves and about their addiction to playing video games. These modules serve as avenues for self-reflection and group experiences revolving around topics of importance in the lives of the participants in the group.

The activities in this workbook are user-friendly and varied to provide a comprehensive way of analyzing, strengthening, and developing characteristics, skills, and attitudes for overcoming an addiction to video games.

The activities, handouts, and assessments in this workbook are completely reproducible and can be photocopied and/or revised for direct participant use.

> https://WholePerson.com/store/TheGamingAddictionWorkbook3219.html

Module 1: My Gaming Addiction

This module helps participants explore their different types of symptoms related to their gaming addiction, amounts of time spent gaming, and how gaming is causing problems at work, in school, with friends and families, and with finances.

Module 2: Develop a New Lifestyle

This module helps participants explore how important it is to investigate and develop a new type of lifestyle, explore and become aware of one's skills and abilities, step up self-esteem, set goals, and find other meaningful, enjoyable activities.

Module 3: Socialization Skills

This module helps participants examine the amount of non-gaming socialization they are currently experiencing, the social skills they lack, ways of becoming more social with people, developing face-to-face relationships, and building on existing relationships.

Module 4: Self-Control

This module helps participants explore how well they are able to control compulsions, impulses, and urges to play video games, how much self-control they currently have, and ways of developing increased willpower, impulse control, and discipline.

Module 5: Healthy Balance

This module helps participants discover ways to promote a healthy and productive future, explore ways that gaming has impaired their lives, develop coping skills, set limits on the amount of time they spend gaming, explore the consequences of their gaming behavior, and ways to make healthier choices.

Different Types of Activity Handouts Included in this Workbook

Some of the various types of materials included in this reproducible workbook:

- **Action Plans** assist participants in meeting the goals and objectives of treatment.

- **Assessments** allow participants to explore their behavior.

- **Case Studies** allow participants the opportunity to share their thoughts about actual cases.

- **Drawing and Doodling** unleash the power of the right side of the brain.

- **Educational Pages** provide insights and tips related to the topic.

- **Group Activities** encourage collaboration among participants and group brainstorming.

- **Journaling Activities** help participants clarify their thoughts and feelings, thus gaining helpful self-knowledge.

- **Positive Affirmations** allow participants to create formidable affirmations that can be posted and repeated to oneself when impulses begin.

- **Quotation Pages** allow participants to reflect on many powerful quotes to think about how they apply to their own life.

- **Rewards Pages** to remind participants to reward themselves as they progress toward their goals.

- **Tables** require participants to reflect on their lives in the past, understand themselves in the present, and react more effectively in the future.

- **And Many More.**

References

American Addiction Centers (2019). Behavioral Addictions.
    https://www.americanaddictioncenters.org/behavioral-addictions

American Medical Association (2007). AMA Considers a New Addiction: Video Games.
    https://www.technologyreview.com/s/408128/ama-considers-a-new-addiction-video-games/

American Psychiatric Association (2018). Diagnostic and Statistical Manual of Mental Disorders (DSM–5).
    https://www.psychiatry.org/psychiatrists/practice/dsm

National Institute of Health (2010). Introduction to Behavioral Addictions.
    https://www.ncbi.nlm.nih.gov/pmc/articles/PMC3164585/

World Health Organization (2018). Gaming Disorder.
    https://www.who.int/features/qa/gaming-disorder/en/

Table of Contents

Table of Contents

(Continued on page xvi)

Table of Contents

© 2021 WHOLE PERSON ASSOCIATES, 101 WEST 2ND STREET, SUITE 203, DULUTH MN 55802 • 800-247-6789 • WHOLEPERSON.COM

My Gaming Addiction

Name _____

Date _____

My Gaming Addiction Assessment
Introduction and Directions

People who are addicted to video games find themselves gaming for inordinate lengths of time. These individuals not only play games every spare minute they have, they play even though it may be causing problems at work, in school, with friends and families, and with finances.

The *My Gaming Addiction Assessment* is designed to help you explore different types of symptoms experienced by people with a gaming addiction. It contains statements that are related to excessive gaming behavior. Read each of the statements and decide if the statement is descriptive of your own gaming behavior.

For each of the items, place a check mark in front of the items that best describe you.

This is not a comprehensive list, but are some of the gaming behaviors that can lead to a video game addiction.

In the following example, the person completing the assessment checked two of three gaming behaviors in which they engaged in excessively:

Since I have been involved in gaming activities...

- ✓ *Others have noticed a decrease in my personal hygiene or grooming.*
- ✓ *I am often unable to think about anything other than gaming.*
- ☐ *I have noticed a decline in my work/school achievement.*

Be honest. No one needs to see this if you do not wish to share.

(Turn to the next page and begin.)

My Gaming Addiction Assessment

Since I have been involved in gaming activities ...

☐ Others have noticed a decrease in my personal hygiene.

☐ I am often unable to think about anything other than gaming.

☐ I have noticed a decline in my work/school achievement.

☐ I have dropped most of my other activities.

☐ Most of my friends are gaming partners.

☐ I feel depressed when I attempt to cut down on the use of video games.

☐ I usually game a little longer than I originally intended.

☐ I have headaches, eye strain, or a sore back from extended game playing.

☐ I do not set limits on how much time I spend gaming.

☐ I am irritable and frustrated when I stop gaming, even for brief periods of time.

☐ I have isolated myself from family and friends in order to develop gaming friends.

☐ I have jeopardized significant relationships because of gaming.

☐ I have risked losing my job or career opportunities because of game play.

☐ I have very few face-to-face social relationships left.

☐ I lie to family members and friends in order to conceal my involvement in gaming.

☐ I feel the need to spend even more time playing games than usual.

☐ I neglect other friendships and activities.

☐ I do not complete my household responsibilities as a result of a preoccupation with gaming.

☐ I have unsuccessfully tried to control, cut back, or stop playing video games.

☐ I feel incomplete physically and/or emotionally if I am unable to game.

☐ I am often unable to accomplish my everyday tasks because of my gaming.

☐ I am tired during the day due to staying up late gaming.

☐ I play games in order to escape from my problems.

☐ I play games as a way to escape stressful situations.

☐ I can no longer control the amount of time I spend playing games.

☐ I think gaming might be dominating my life.

☐ I feel a compulsion to play games.

☐ I become furious when I am told to stop gaming.

☐ I am irritable when I don't have time to play video games.

☐ I find that I have little in common with friends who do not play video games.

Number of items checked = _____

(Go to Scoring Directions on the next page.)

My Gaming Addiction Assessment
Scoring Directions & Profile Interpretations

The assessment you just completed is designed to measure the extent to which you are engaging in various addictive gaming behaviors.

Count the number of items you checked on the My Gaming Addiction Assessment. Put that total on the line marked TOTAL at the end of the section on the assessment. Then, transfer your total to this space below:

Number of items check marked = _____

~~~~~~

Assessment Profile Interpretation

If you checked even one item, you are at risk for developing or having a gaming addiction. The more items you checked, the greater the risk.

My Gaming Addiction Total _____

This assessment measures the extent of your excessive gaming behavior.

Remember that even one checked item can suggest you are experiencing a gaming-related addiction. The HIGHER your score on the My Gaming Addiction Assessment, the greater the extent of your gaming addiction.

What surprises you about your score?_____

_____

How did any of the items you checked off cause you to think about changing your actions?

_____

_____

What steps can you immediately take to reduce the time you are spending gaming?

_____

_____

My Video Game Time

Often, people do not realize the amount of time they spend on gaming. By completing this chart, you will become aware of the amount of time you spend on gaming. You do not need to share this with anyone.

For one week, every day, complete this chart.

Days of the Week	Game(s) Played	Started	Stopped	Total Hours
Monday				
Tuesday				
Wednesday				
Thursday				
Friday				
Saturday				
Sunday				

Which games did you play the most? _____

_____

How many hours did you play this week? _____

What didn't you do because of the gaming? _____

_____

_____

Who was disappointed in you because of the time you spent gaming? _____

_____

_____

Time to Cut Back?

Regardless of how much time you are spending each week to play video games, it is a good idea to cut back. When cutting back, it is important to go slowly and cut back gradually, not all at once. If you are currently gaming 30 hours per week, you may want to cut back to 27 next week, 25 the following week, etc. This will allow you to become more conscious of how much time you are engaged in the activity and slowly wean yourself down to a realistic amount of time you spend playing video games.

The approximate number of hours I spend gaming during a typical week _____.

WEEK 1: How I cut down on my gaming: _____

_____

    Total amount of time I spent this week after cutting down:_____

    My reaction to cutting down: _____

    _____

WEEK 2: How I cut down on my gaming: _____

_____

    Total amount of time I spent this week after cutting down:_____

    My reaction to cutting down: _____

    _____

WEEK 3: How I cut down on my gaming: _____

_____

    Total amount of time I spent this week after cutting down:_____

    My reaction to cutting down: _____

    _____

WEEK 4: How I cut down on my gaming: _____

_____

    Total amount of time I spent this week after cutting down:_____

    My reaction to cutting down: _____

    _____

WEEK 5: How I cut down on my gaming: _____

_____

    Total amount of time I spent this week after cutting down:_____

    My reaction to cutting down: _____

    _____

TOTAL HOURS A week spent gaming after cutting down: _____

Controlling My Own Life

When you have a video game addiction, you probably find that gaming starts to control your life. If it is creating stress, jeopardizing your career, interfering with your personal relationships, causing physical and emotional problems, and/or causing financial hardships, gaming is controlling your life.

In the spaces below, investigate how gaming may be controlling your life:

Aspects of My Life	How Gaming is Controlling My Life	What I Need to Repair
Example: *Creating Stress*	*I feel like I need to game all the time, and I become miserable when I'm not gaming.*	*I need to find some substitute activities to engage in rather than gaming all the time.*
Creating Stress		
Jeopardizing My Career		
Interfering with Relationships		
Physical and/or Emotional Problems		
Causing Financial Problems		
Other		

> ***It is important to remember that you are in control, not the video games!***
> ***It is your responsibility to control how and when you play video games.***

You need to start by:
- Setting aside specific starting and ending times of the day you will play your favorite video game.
- Finding alternatives to gaming.
- Developing social relationships with people outside of your gaming circle

Pre-Occupied?

Pre-occupation: an idea or subject that someone thinks about most of the time, or an extreme or excessive concern with something.

Do you spend a lot of time thinking about games even when you are not playing? Do you constantly plan when you can play next? When do you do this the most?

In the spaces below, identify when you become pre-occupied with playing video games.
Example: I wanted to be close with O.F.L. but he was always gaming, so I joined him.

It is preoccupation with possessions, more than anything else,
that prevents us from living freely and nobly.
~ Bertrand Russell

Deception?

Deception: the act of causing someone to accept as true
or valid what is false or invalid.

Do you lie to family, friends, or others about how much you game? Do you try to keep your family or friends from knowing how much you game?

In the circles below, write about how you have deceived people in order to play video games.

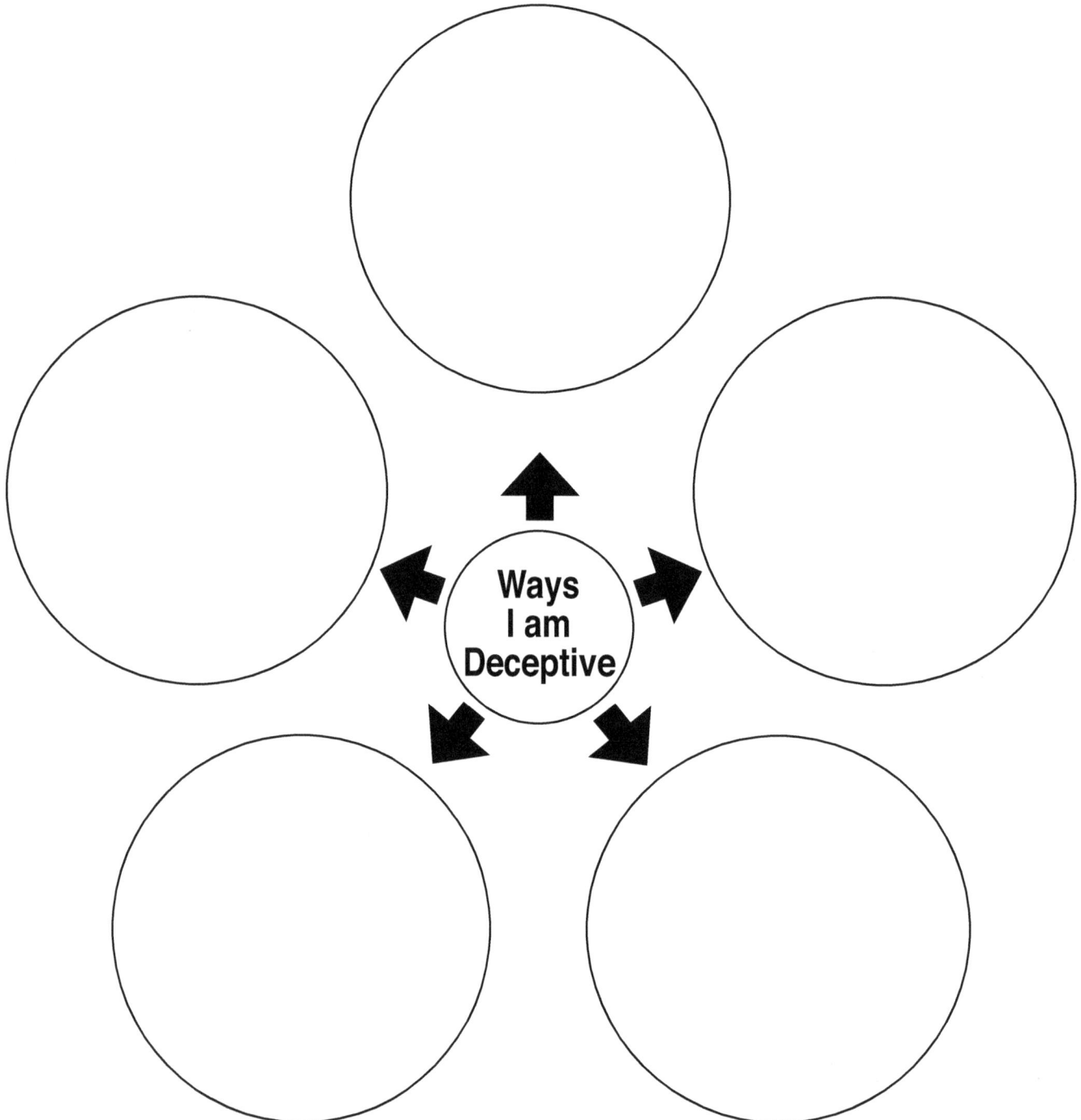

**Ways
I am
Deceptive**

© 2021 WHOLE PERSON ASSOCIATES, 101 WEST 2ND STREET, SUITE 203, DULUTH MN 55802 • 800-247-6789 • WHOLEPERSON.COM

Continue Despite Problems?

Do you continue to play games even though you are aware of negative consequences? *Example: not getting enough sleep, being late to school/work, spending too much money, failing classes, not attending meetings, having arguments with others, or neglecting important duties.*

Below, identify the problems you are experiencing because of game play. Be Honest!

Problems I Have Encountered ⇨ **Why I Continue to Game**

_____ ⇨ _____

_____ ⇨ _____

_____ ⇨ _____

_____ ⇨ _____

_____ ⇨ _____

_____ ⇨ _____

_____ ⇨ _____

A change in bad habits leads to a change in life.
~ Jenny Craig

What does the above quote mean to you?

_____

_____

_____

Withdraw?

Withdraw: to remove from consideration or set outside a group.

Do you feel restless, irritable, moody, angry, anxious or sad when attempting to cut down or stop gaming, or when you are unable to play?

In the spaces below, explore the times you have tried to withdraw from gaming:

Times I Tried to Withdraw	The Way I Reacted	Healthy Activities I Did or Could Have Substituted for Gaming
Example: *Last Sunday night*	*I became irritable and even nasty with the people I work with.*	*I could have exercised at the gym with some of my friends before going to work.*

**No one is immune from addiction; it afflicts people
of all ages, races, classes, and professions.**
~ Patrick J. Kennedy

Incredible Change Happens

Think about the following quote, and then write about your answers to the questions that follow the quote.

Incredible change happens in your life when you decide to take control of what you do have power over instead of craving control over what you don't.
~ Steve Maraboli

Do you agree with the author? Why or why not?

_____

_____

_____

What changes do you want to see in your life?

_____

_____

_____

How will you take control of your gaming addiction?

_____

_____

_____

What do you have the power to control in your addiction to playing video games?

_____

_____

_____

Who are some trusted people in your life you can talk with who will support you in significant change?

_____

_____

_____

Why Do You Play Video Games?

Many people do not know why they play video games. They believe that games are enjoyable, and a fun way to pass the time. By thinking about it, and the issues that arise because of it, they recognize that they are gaming for many reasons other than enjoyment.

Take some time to really reflect on WHY you play video games. Some possible reasons are listed below. Why do you play? How do you think this helps you? How can you achieve the same benefits you believe you get from playing without the games?

Reasons people play:
- To be in a place where they are not judged.
- To block out their negative emotions or mood.
- To escape from their problems.
- To feel accepted.
- To have a connection with the online video community.
- To have feelings of achievement.
- To reduce stress.

Why I Play Video Games	How It Helps Me	How Can I Achieve the Same Benefits Without the Games?
Example: To meet other people who have the same interests as I do.	*It keeps me from being socially isolated and so angry.*	*Join another type of club or activity in my community where I could meet like-minded people.*

What are the Risks in Gaming?

People risk or lose significant relationships, a job, educational or career opportunities because of gaming!

In the spaces that follow, write, doodle, or draw pictures of situations or people you may be risking, or have already lost, in your life.

Have You Given Up Other Activities?

Have you reduced your participation in other recreational activities due to gaming?

Below, write about the activities you have given up because of your gaming.

I have given up _____

because _____

_____

_____

_____

I have given up _____

because _____

_____

_____

_____

I have given up _____

because _____

_____

_____

_____

I have given up _____

because _____

_____

_____

_____

© 2021 WHOLE PERSON ASSOCIATES, 101 WEST 2ND STREET, SUITE 203, DULUTH MN 55802 • 800-247-6789 • WHOLEPERSON.COM

My Gaming Behaviors

This page will help you to explore your behaviors related to gaming.

Answer each sentence fragment by writing about your own experiences with gaming.

I started gaming when _____

_____

_____

My gaming addiction first started because_____

_____

_____

I first realized I had a gaming problem when _____

_____

_____

I game most when I am _____

_____

_____

The time(s) of day when I game the most are_____

_____

_____

Gaming has affected my life by _____

_____

_____

My favorite place to game is _____

_____

_____

I have tried to quit and _____

_____

_____

I will make a promise to try to quit by _____

_____

_____

Some things I can do instead of gaming are _____

_____

_____

My Impulse Control

Impulsivity: failure to resist a temptation, an urge, an impulse,
or the inability to not speak on a thought.

Think about your gaming behaviors, and describe your control impulses below:

I am able/unable to control how much time I spend playing games.

Gaming tends to dominate my life.

I feel driven to play video games.

I can't control the desire to keep playing games longer to get a bigger thrill and win.

The Serenity Prayer

Grant me the serenity to accept the things I cannot change,
Courage to change the things I can, And wisdom to know the difference.

What are YOUR Gaming Triggers?

For people addicted to gaming, it is vital to recognize the people, places, and situations that trigger your need to play video games. Once you have identified your triggers, you can take action to manage and ignore the triggers when they occur.

My Triggers	Action I Can Take to Manage Them
Example: Stress at work	*Join a martial arts class and practice when I feel the urge to game.*
Example: My friend emails and asks me to play.	*I need to think about things I need to do and people in my life who want me to be with them or to help them.*

What's Important in Your Life?

Some of the reasons people enjoy playing video games as much as they do is because it can be rewarding, fun, and offers a level of social interactivity with other players in the game. However, it is extremely important to prioritize what's important in your life: Friends? Family? Career? Watching or going to sports events? Educational endeavors? Getting to the gym? Social activities? Good movies?

Below, identify the important people and things in your life other than gaming, rank them in order, and write about why you ranked them as you did.

Important People & Things in My life	Why These People or Things are Important to Me	Rank Order

What did you learn about yourself from this activity? _____

_____

Quotes about Gaming Addictions

On the lines that follow each of the quotations,
describe what the quotation means to you and how it applies to YOUR life.

Video games and computers have become babysitters for kids.
~ Taylor Kitsch

_____

_____

_____

I play video games a lot... I love to read... I enjoy spending time with my
husband and daughter, who are my most favorite people in the world.
~ Lea Salonga

_____

_____

_____

If you don't know someone who's had a problem with addiction, you will.
~ Dana Boente

_____

_____

_____

There is a quality of selfishness that is associated with an individual
when they are in the depths of addiction.
~ David Dastmalchian

_____

_____

_____

Which quote especially speaks to you and your gaming addiction? Why?

_____

_____

_____

39

Gaming

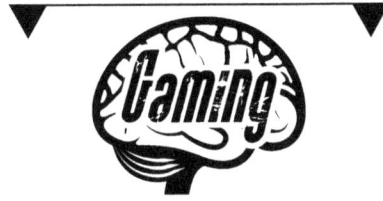

Develop a New Lifestyle

Name _____

Date _____

New Lifestyle Assessment
Introduction and Directions

To overcome excessive gaming, it is important to investigate and develop a new type of lifestyle. To do this, it is helpful to explore and become aware of one's skills and abilities, step up self-esteem, set goals, and find other meaningful, enjoyable activities.

The *New Lifestyle Assessment* is designed to explore various ways to develop a new lifestyle. It contains statements that are divided into four lifestyle categories. Read each of the statements and decide if and how each one is descriptive of you.

In each of the choices listed, circle the number of your response on the line to the right of each statement. In the following example, the circled 1 indicates the statement is UNLIKE the person completing the inventory:

	LIKE ME	UNLIKE ME
Related to my lifestyle ...		
I have skills that I am not using...	2	(1)

(Turn to the next page and begin.)

New Lifestyle Assessment

Name _____ Date _____

	LIKE ME	UNLIKE ME

Related to my lifestyle ...

	LIKE ME	UNLIKE ME
I have skills that I am not using.	2	1
I am aware that I am not living up to my full potential.	2	1
I game because I am bored at work/school.	2	1
I don't know how to go about developing my other abilities.	2	1
I haven't found something I like or do as well as I game.	2	1

I. TOTAL = _____

Related to my lifestyle ...

	LIKE ME	UNLIKE ME
I have a difficult time feeling good about myself.	2	1
I feel rejected easily.	2	1
I often feel like a failure.	2	1
I am critical of myself.	2	1
I rarely acknowledge any successes other than gaming.	2	1

II. TOTAL = _____

Related to my lifestyle ...

	LIKE ME	UNLIKE ME
I have no long-term personal goals.	2	1
I have no long-term professional goals.	2	1
I am not motivated to work toward a goal other than gaming.	2	1
I lack an action plan to attain an education-related goal.	2	1
I let setbacks deter me.	2	1

III. TOTAL = _____

Related to my lifestyle ...

	LIKE ME	UNLIKE ME
I lack healthy alternatives to gaming.	2	1
All I am motivated to do is play video games.	2	1
I don't have friends to do things with.	2	1
At times, I can't think about doing anything else but gaming.	2	1
Nothing provides me with the high I get from gaming.	2	1

IV. TOTAL = _____

(Continue on the next page for the scale descriptions and profile interpretations)

New Lifestyle Assessment

Name (use a name code)_____ Date _____

Scoring Directions & Profile Interpretations

The New Lifestyle Assessment is designed to measure the effects that gaming has on your everyday life. (If left unchecked, it can negatively affect the brain, memory, and vision, as well as lead to stress, anxiety, and even isolation if the addiction gets severe enough.)

On the previous page, count the scores you circled for each of the four sections. Put that total on the line marked "Total" at the end of each section. Transfer your totals to the spaces below:

    I.   **Skills & Abilities Total**   = _____

    II. **Self-Esteem Total**   = _____

    III. **Set Goals Total**   = _____

    IV. **Alternatives Total**   = _____

~~~~~~

Assessment Profile Interpretation

In each of the sections, place an X on the line to note your score.

SCALE I – Skills & Abilities: This scale measures the use of your skills and abilities other than games.

_____
5 = Low   **8 = Moderate**   **10 = High**

SCALE I – Self-Esteem: This scale measures how you feel about yourself.

_____
5 = Low   **8 = Moderate**   **10 = High**

SCALE III – Set Goals: This scale measures how you set and work toward goals.

_____
5 = Low   **8 = Moderate**   **10 = High**

SCALE IV – Alternatives: This scale measures your alternatives to playing video games.

_____
5 = Low   **8 = Moderate**   **10 = High**

Remember that even one "LIKE ME" score on any of the scales can suggest you are experiencing some effects from a gaming addiction. Areas in which you scored LOW on the above profile interpretation can suggest that you are not experiencing many signs of a gaming addiction. The HIGHER your score on each of the scales, the more of a video-game problem you have in the specific aspect measured by the assessment.

What I Used to Love to Do

It is important to search various aspects of your life for the things you used to love to do. By examining what you have truly enjoyed doing, you can identify some of the things you can still do.

Spend some time thinking about what you loved and why you loved these activities. If you can't remember what you used to love to do, ask someone who knows you well who can remind you. Try to find two examples of each.

For example, at school or work you may have enjoyed tutoring or mentoring others, while at home you may have found it to be relaxing when listening to classical music. You may have loved to read a new book that was just released or take a walk with your pet.

Finish the sentence starters below:

At home, I loved to _____

_____

At home, I loved to _____

_____

At work, I loved to _____

_____

At work, I loved to _____

_____

In my spare time, I loved to _____

_____

In my spare time, I loved to _____

_____

When I was with others, I loved to _____

_____

When I was with others, I loved to _____

_____

When I felt creative, I loved to _____

_____

When I felt creative, I loved to _____

_____

How can you resume some of the things that you once loved to do? _____

_____

_____

Skills & Abilities

Other than playing video games, what are you really good at? All people have hidden skills and abilities they stopped using or have never fully used.

What are your hidden skills and abilities? For example, you may be great at writing, or you may have excelled at history in school, or you might be excellent at a sport or exercise.

Write about, draw, or doodle your hidden skills and abilities in the boxes below:

In my job, I am very good at …	In school, I was very good at …
Why I am good at this …	Why I was good at this …
When I volunteer or help others, I …	In my spare time, I used to …
Why I was good at this …	Why I stopped doing this …

It's a shame to let your skills and abilities go to waste! How can you continue to use these skills and abilities some of the time?

_____

_____

_____

My Core Competencies

It is time to identify your core competencies and begin to develop them further. Self-esteem is built by demonstrating real ability and achievement in areas that matter. If you pride yourself on being a good cook, you could have more dinner parties. If you enjoy running, you could sign up for races and train for them. Think about your competencies and find opportunities to develop and engage in them. This will help you develop greater self-esteem and can be a substitute for things you do way too much, or to substitute for the behavioral addictions you have developed.

Complete the table that follows to identify your core competencies.

Core Competency	How It Will Develop Greater Self-Esteem	How It Will Limit the Amount of Time I Play Video Games
Example: Drawing caricatures.	I feel good when being creative.	I will draw before bed rather than gaming.

Self-esteem comes quietly, like the truth.
~ Amity Gaige

Symptoms of Low Self-Esteem

Many people feel that playing video games is the only way for them to feel good about themselves.

On the line under each symptom of low self-esteem, place an X on the continuum of how much you relate to the statement. On the dotted line below each one, write why you rated yourself that way. Be HONEST!

Once I begin I do not realize how much time I spend gaming.

0 (Not Like Me)   5 (Somewhat Like Me)   10 (Much Like Me)

. . . .

When I am not gaming, I feel anxious.

0 (Not Like Me)   5 (Somewhat Like Me)   10 (Much Like Me)

. . . .

Gaming is my only social contact.

0 (Not Like Me)   5 (Somewhat Like Me)   10 (Much Like Me)

. . . .

When I am not gaming, I treat myself and others badly.

0 (Not Like Me)   5 (Somewhat Like Me)   10 (Much Like Me)

. . . .

I don't feel fulfilled unless I am gaming.

0 (Not Like Me)   5 (Somewhat Like Me)   10 (Much Like Me)

. . . .

I'm not good at anything else but gaming.

0 (Not Like Me)   5 (Somewhat Like Me)   10 (Much Like Me)

. . . .

The HIGHER Much Like Me scores on each of the statements indicates that you have a gaming addiction. Somewhat Like Me scores other than getting a 0 can be indicative of a gaming addiction problem. Areas where you scored lower Not Like Me suggest that you are not experiencing many signs of a gaming problem in those areas but indicate that you need to be careful.

When I Feel Good About Myself

People addicted to video games often feel like they are not good at anything else. They don't feel good about themselves unless they are gaming. It is critical to explore what else triggers your self-esteem. Other than when playing video games, think about the places (work, home, park, etc.), situations (fixing computers, learning languages, etc.), or other people (NKY whom I mentor at work) that seem to positively impact how you feel about yourself.

Below, identify some of the places, situations, and people that trigger good feelings about yourself.

Places
1. _____
2. _____
3. _____

Situations
1. _____
2. _____
3. _____

People
1. _____
2. _____
3. _____

How can you spend more time (not gaming!) with places, situations, and people that boost your self-esteem? Choose one of the places, situations, and people you identified in each of the boxes above and, on the lines below, write about how you will increase your involvement with each of them you identified.

Places_____

_____

_____

Situations _____

_____

_____

People _____

_____

_____

© 2021 WHOLE PERSON ASSOCIATES, 101 WEST 2ND STREET, SUITE 203, DULUTH MN 55802 • 800-247-6789 • WHOLEPERSON.COM

Celebrate the Small Stuff

Celebrating small victories is a great way to build confidence and start feeling better about yourself. Small victories are often overlooked.

For example,
- *You made yourself two eggs for breakfast.*
- *You took a hike and walked a half-mile.*
- *You helped someone move some furniture.*

For a week, track and celebrate your small victories not related to gaming.

Days of the Week	My Small Victories
Monday	
Tuesday	
Wednesday	
Thursday	
Friday	
Saturday	
Sunday	

Copy this page and use it to track your small victories over multiple weeks.

© 2021 WHOLE PERSON ASSOCIATES, 101 WEST 2ND STREET, SUITE 203, DULUTH MN 55802 • 800-247-6789 • WHOLEPERSON.COM

My Goals

If you want to succeed in life, you need to set and work toward goals. Without goals, you lack motivation, focus, and direction. Goal setting allows you to take control of your life's direction and provides you a benchmark for determining whether you are actually succeeding.

Here are some general rules for goal setting:

To be effective, your goals must be **SMART**. SMART is an acronym for:

  S (Specific)   Goals should be concise and clearly defined.
  M (Measurable)   Goals should have a tangible result that can be measured.
  A (Attainable)   Goals should be achievable, yet challenging to you.
  R (Realistic)   Goals should represent an objective toward which you will work.
  T (Time Oriented) Goals should link to a time frame to create a sense of urgency.

Set some goals for overcoming an addiction to playing video games.

Goals (Be specific)	Measuring the Goals	By When?
Example: *Reduce the hours spent gaming each day.*	*I will reduce my gaming from 6 to 4 hours per day.*	*By the end of the month.*

Rank the goals as to their importance.

My Personal Life Goals

If you want to succeed in overcoming an addiction, you need to set and work toward personal life goals. Personal life goals might include such things as making a non-addicted new friend, joining a chess club, developing a support network, etc.

Here are some general rules for goal setting (the same ones you used in the Goals worksheet):

To be effective, your goals must be **SMART**. SMART is an acronym for:
> **S (Specific)**   Goals should be concise and clearly defined.
> **M (Measurable)**   Goals should have a tangible result that can be measured.
> **A (Attainable)**   Goals should be achievable, yet challenging to you.
> **R (Realistic)**   Goals should represent an objective toward which you will work.
> **T (Time Oriented)** Goals should link to a time frame to create a sense of urgency.

Set some goals for overcoming an addiction to playing video games.

Goals (Be specific)	Measuring the Goals	By When?
Example: *Host a get-together in* *my neighborhood.*	*I will send an invitation out to 10 people in my neighborhood.*	*Next week.*

Rank the goals as to their importance.

My Work/Volunteer Life Goals

If you want to succeed in overcoming an addiction, you need to set and work toward succeeding at your job and/or volunteer life goals. These life goals might include such things as going to or returning to college for a master's degree, learning a second language, taking a certification course, working more hours, etc.

Here are some general rules for goal setting (the same ones you used in the two previous worksheets):

To be effective, your goals must be **SMART**. SMART is an acronym for:
- **S (Specific)** Goals should be concise and clearly defined.
- **M (Measurable)** Goals should have a tangible result that can be measured.
- **A (Attainable)** Goals should be achievable, yet challenging to you.
- **R (Realistic)** Goals should represent an objective toward which you will work.
- **T (Time Oriented)** Goals should link to a time frame to create a sense of urgency.

Set some goals for overcoming an addiction to playing video games.

Goals (Be specific)	Measuring the Goals	By When?
Example: *Write a pamphlet about management principles.*	*I will complete a proposal for the pamphlet.*	*In six weeks.*

Rank the goals as to their importance.

Breaking Down My Addiction Goals

Goals can be overwhelming. The goal of reducing and ultimately eliminating your need to play video games is a HUGE goal! One of the keys to achieving these types of major goals is to break them into mini-goals. When you achieve these mini-goals, you receive the motivation and vision to achieve larger, more important goals. When you are focused on your goals that are not related to playing video games, you will be better able to cope with the urge to game.

For your goal of reducing the amount of time you are playing video games, set some mini-goals that you can work on daily to reach your major goal. To do so, think backwards and describe the mini-goals you would need to reach in order to achieve your major goal.

For Example: my mini-goals:
1. *Make several friends in person.*
2. *Join a gym and begin exercising.*
3. *Start reading a book each month.*
4. *Take a management class.*
5. *Learn to meditate.*

My mini-goals:

1. _____

   _____

2. _____

   _____

3. _____

   _____

4. _____

   _____

5. _____

   _____

What you get by achieving your goals is not as important
as what you become by achieving your goals.
~ Zig Ziglar

Goals and Plans

If you go to work on your goals, your goals will go to work on you.
If you go to work on your plan, your plan will go to work on you.
Whatever good things we build end up building us.
~ Jim Rohn

What does the above quote mean to you?

_____

_____

_____

What goal or plan are you willing to work on to reduce your addiction to playing video games?

_____

_____

_____

How do you think that reducing your addiction to gaming will change you?

_____

_____

_____

How do you think that by reducing your addiction to gaming your relationships at home will change?

_____

_____

_____

How do you think that by reducing your addiction to gaming your work or volunteer relationships will change?

_____

_____

_____

How do you think that successfully ENDING your addiction to gaming would change your life?

_____

_____

_____

Activities and People I've Given Up

A FACT: When addicted to playing video games, people often give up many activities and people in order to have the time, money, or interest to play. Because of this fact, the addiction becomes even stronger. It is vital to live a full life by engaging with people and activities that provide you with joy and contentment, not dependent on gaming together.

In each section below, identify the people and activities you have given up:

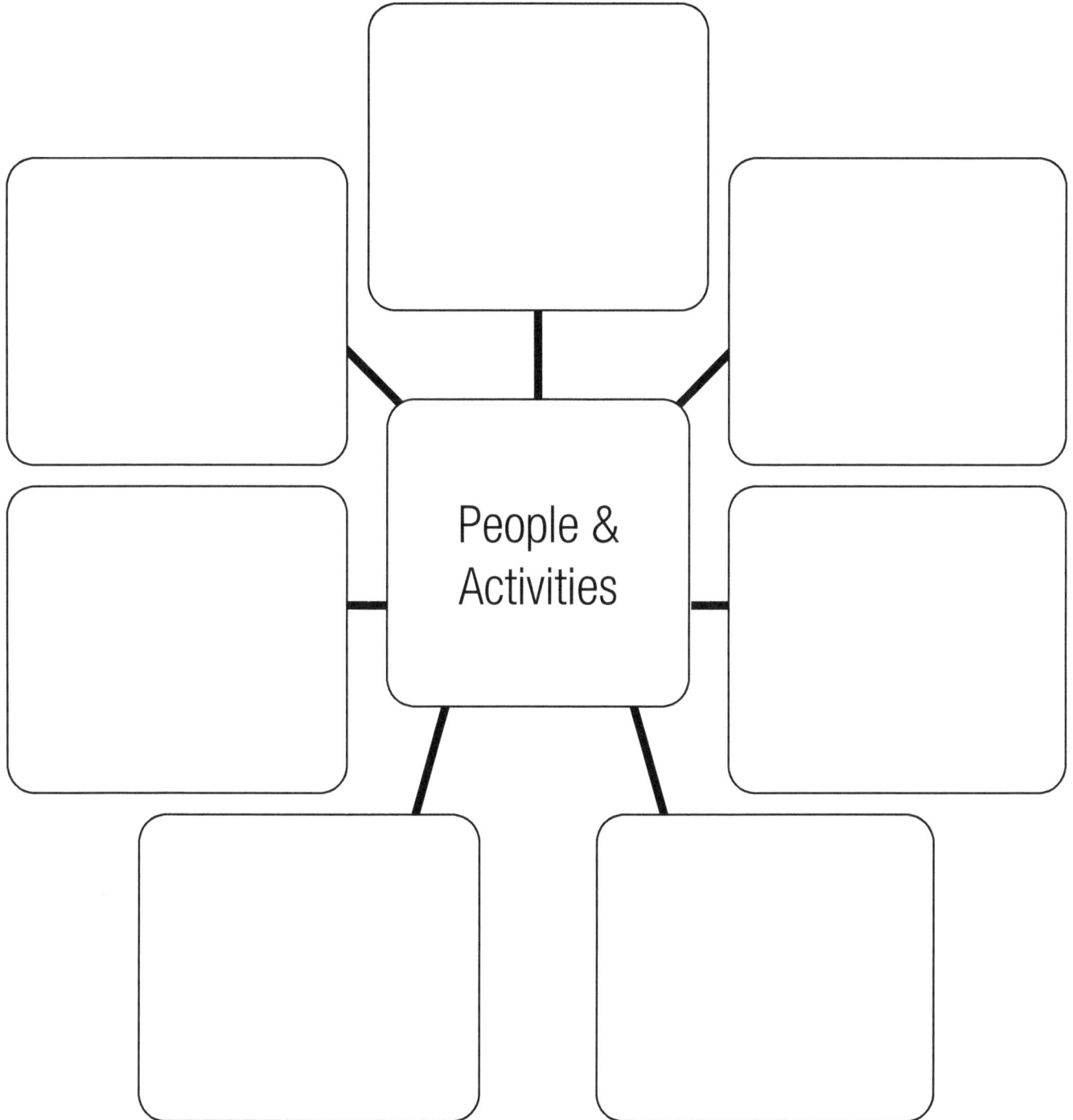

People & Activities

What surprises you about the list of activities and people you generated?

Relaxing My Mind and Body (Page 1)

People with a gaming problem get bored easily when they are doing something other than gaming. They find their minds racing and their bodies filling with anxiety. It is important to learn some tools and techniques for relaxing your mind and body.

When you are not gaming, and you need to relax, try these.

Alternative 1 - Reduce physical tension by taking a deep breath and holding it for five seconds. Breathe in through your nose and exhale through your mouth. Do this at least ten more times. How did that feel?

_____

_____

_____

_____

Alternative 2 - Be mindful by bringing your thoughts to the here-and-now (as if the future does not exist!). Stop thinking about gaming in the past and your desire to game in the future, and think about something else to look forward to. How did that feel?

_____

_____

_____

_____

Alternative 3 - Visualize a mental image of a calm place like the beach or walking in the woods. Close your eyes and picture yourself in this calm place. Use your senses of smell, touch, taste, and hearing to make the image real. How did that feel?

_____

_____

_____

_____

Alternative 4 - Calm your body in order to achieve a sense of deep relaxation. Start at the bottom of your feet and begin relaxing all of your muscles until you reach the top of your head. Say to yourself, "I can feel my feet starting to relax, now my calves are relaxing, etc." How did that feel?

_____

_____

_____

_____

(Continued on the Next Page)

Relaxing My Mind and Body (Page 2)

Alternative 5 - Think realistically by truthfully assessing the accuracy and rationality of the thoughts you are thinking. This process is called self-reflection. Stop any negative statements and replace them with positive statements. How did that feel?

_____

_____

_____

_____

Alternative 6 - Be positive by repeating several positive affirmations that will help you to stay in the present moment. Affirmations might include statements such as "My thinking is peace-filled, I will be okay if I am not gaming. I can enjoy many other activities and people rather than playing video games." How did that feel?

_____

_____

_____

_____

Alternative 7 - Be soothed by listening to relaxing music. Think of the types of music, or specific pieces or songs that help you to relax and feel soothed. How did that feel?

_____

_____

_____

_____

Alternative 8 - Be active by engaging in exercise, running, jogging, yoga, etc. These types of active, movement-based practices can keep your mind focused. How did that feel?

_____

_____

_____

_____

Which alternative activities did you try and how successful were they?

_____

_____

_____

_____

Activities that FLOW!

According to positive psychologist Mihály Csíkszentmihályi, flow is a state of complete immersion in an activity. He describes the mental state of flow as being completely involved in an activity for its own sake. The ego falls away. Time flies. Every action, movement, and thought follows inevitably from the previous one, like playing jazz. Your whole being is involved, and you're using your skills to the utmost.

It is vital that people addicted to playing video games find alternatives that flow. What hobbies, activities, or tasks occupy your full attention (other than gaming) so much so that you are completely engaged in the present moment? You think that no time has passed, look at the clock, and poof! Three hours have gone by! These things can be related to your job, education, spare-time, time with friends, movies, time with children, etc.

Below, identify those activities and what you love about them, what keeps you so engaged in them, and how you can do them more.

An Activity I Love	What I Love About It	Why It Keeps Me Engaged	How I Can Do it More
Example: Playing chess	*It requires the use of strategy.*	*It requires even more strategy than most video games.*	*I can make a date with my Dad to play once a week. He would be thrilled!*

© 2021 WHOLE PERSON ASSOCIATES, 101 WEST 2ND STREET, SUITE 203, DULUTH MN 55802 • 800-247-6789 • WHOLEPERSON.COM

Quotes about Developing a New Lifestyle

*On the lines that follow each of the quotes, describe what the
quote means to you and how it applies to YOUR life.*

When it is obvious that the goals cannot be reached,
don't adjust the goals, adjust the action steps.
~ Confucius

_____

_____

_____

Self-esteem is as important to our well-being as legs are to a table.
It is essential for physical and mental health and for happiness.
~ Louise Hart

_____

_____

_____

Strength does not come from winning. Your struggles develop your strengths.
When you go through hardships and decide not to surrender, that is strength.
~ Arnold Schwarzenegger

_____

_____

_____

Which quote especially speaks to you and your plan to develop a new lifestyle? Why?

_____

_____

_____

_____

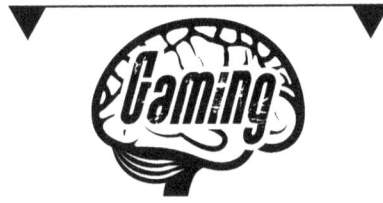

Socialization Skills

Name _____

Date _____

© 2021 WHOLE PERSON ASSOCIATES, 101 WEST 2ND STREET, SUITE 203, DULUTH MN 55802 • 800-247-6789 • WHOLEPERSON.COM

Non-Gaming Face-to-Face Socialization Assessment
Introduction and Directions

People who become addicted to playing video games often get caught in a vicious cycle where they usually lack social skills. They play video games in lieu of taking social risks and then fail to develop those skills because they do not engage enough socially in their lives.

The following assessment contains 18 statements related to the social aspects of your life. This assessment can help you to gauge the amount of non-gaming socialization you are currently experiencing. Read each of the statements and decide whether or not the statement describes you.

If the statement describes you, circle the number in the YES column next to that item.
If the statement does not describe you, circle the number in the NO column next to that item.

In the following example, the circled 2 indicates that the person completing this assessment believes that the statement describes him or her:

	YES	NO

When it comes to non-gaming face-to-face social relationships...
I would rather interact with people online. . . . .(2). 1

This is not a test. Since there are no right or wrong answers, do not spend too much time thinking about your answers. Be sure to respond to every statement.

(Turn to the next page and begin.)

Non-Gaming Face-to-Face Socialization Assessment

Name _____ Date _____

	YES	NO
When it comes to non-gaming face-to-face social relationships...		
I would rather interact with people online.	2	1
I feel unworthy of friendships and loyalty of others.	2	1
I prefer gaming rather than just being with people.	2	1
I have difficulty maintaining healthy personal relationships.	2	1
I neglect my friends and family.	2	1
I feel alone and lonely.	2	1

Relationships TOTAL = _____

	YES	NO
With regard to non-gaming face-to-face social situations...		
I avoid social situations.	2	1
I never join in the conversations.	2	1
I find it hard to approach people.	2	1
I try to meet new people.	2	1
I am afraid of being rejected by others.	2	1
I often feel left out.	2	1

Isolation TOTAL = _____

	YES	NO
When I am in non-gaming face-to-face social situations...		
I am afraid of making stupid mistakes.	2	1
I worry that others will laugh at me.	2	1
I fear that I will embarrass myself.	2	1
I talk too much about gaming.	2	1
I feel awkward.	2	1
I am pretty sure I will at some point embarrass or hurt someone.	2	1

Awkwardness TOTAL = _____

(Go to the next page for the scoring assessment results, profile interpretation, and individual descriptions)

Non-Gaming Face-to-Face Socialization Assessment

Name (use a name code)_____ Date _____

Scores & Profile Interpretations

The assessment you just completed is designed to measure the ways you socialize with people face-to-face when you are not gaming.

In each of the sections on the previous page, count the scores you circled. Enter that number on the line marked TOTAL at the end of each section. Transfer your total to the space below, and place an X on the line representing your score.

Relationships = _____ (Your willingness to engage in relationships with people face-to-face.)

_____
6 = Low   **9 = Moderate**   **12 = High**

Isolation = _____ (Your ability to meet people and develop relationships face-to-face.)

_____
6 = Low   **9 = Moderate**   **12 = High**

Awkwardness = _____ (Your feelings of comfort in social situations.)

_____
6 = Low   **9 = Moderate**   **12 = High**

Socialization Assessment Profile Interpretation

Individual Scale Scores	Results	Indications
6 to 7 in any single area	Low	Low scores indicate that you have a limited amount of socialization with non-gaming people, face-to-face.
8 to 10 in any single area	Moderate	Moderate scores indicate that have some amount of socialization with non-gaming people, face-to-face.
11 to 12 in any single area	High	High scores indicate that you have a lot of effective socialization with non-gaming people, face-to-face.

Remember that even one circled item on a scale can suggest you are experiencing a lack of socialization with non-gaming face-to-face people in your life.

The **LOWER** your score on the Social Engagement Assessment, the greater the effect your gaming addiction is having on your social relationships.

Social Consequences Case Study

People addicted to video games are often unable to form and sustain intimate relationships and/or close friendships.

Read the following case study and answer the questions that follow.

> The cell phone of HLC rings and it is his best friend calling. His friend left a message that his grandmother needed a ride to urgent care. HLC thinks about picking up the phone, but he is in the middle of a video game. HLC decides to call him as soon as he is finished with the game.

Describe a time when this type of thing has happened to you.

_____

_____

_____

Do you believe that HLC made a good decision?

_____

_____

_____

What would you have done in this situation?

_____

_____

_____

What should HLC have done in this situation?

_____

_____

_____

Does HLC need to make amends for the decision? If so, how?

_____

_____

_____

Who have you let down because of your addiction to video games?

_____

_____

_____

_____

Ruining Relationships

An addiction to playing video games often ruins relationships. Write the ways that your gaming addiction has put a strain on your relationships. Place a check mark in the boxes of statements that apply to you, and journal about how they have affected your relationships. Write the NAME CODE of each person you are referring to.

☐ **I lost _ _ _'s trust when** _____

_____

_____

☐ **I made _ _ _ angry when** _____

_____

_____

☐ **I kept a secrets from _ _ _ and _ _ _** _____

_____

_____

☐ **I lied to _ _ _ and _ _ _** _____

_____

_____

☐ **I had a meltdown when _ _ _ told me she wouldn't go out with me anymore**

if I didn't stop gaming. _____

_____

_____

☐ **I become angry and aggressive when _ _ _ won't let me** _____

_____

_____

☐ **I neglect _ _ _ when I** _____

_____

_____

☐ **I forget important events when I get caught up with** _____

_____

_____

☐ **Other:** _____

_____

_____

Insecure?

Many people who excessively play video games tend to feel insecure about themselves in social situations. Some of these insecurities are listed below.

On the line under each of the social insecurities listed below, place an X on the continuum of how much you relate to the statement. On the dotted line below each one, write why you rated yourself that way. Be HONEST!

I don't have fun in social situations.

0 (Not Like Me)   5 (Somewhat Like Me)   10 (Much Like Me)

. . . .

I feel like it's my fault when people are disinterested in me.

0 (Not Like Me)   5 (Somewhat Like Me)   10 (Much Like Me)

. . . .

I am afraid of being rejected.

0 (Not Like Me)   5 (Somewhat Like Me)   10 (Much Like Me)

. . . .

I find it difficult to approach people.

0 (Not Like Me)   5 (Somewhat Like Me)   10 (Much Like Me)

. . . .

I can't figure out how to gracefully join in on a conversation.

0 (Not Like Me)   5 (Somewhat Like Me)   10 (Much Like Me)

. . . .

I constantly feel the need to brag about myself.

0 (Not Like Me)   5 (Somewhat Like Me)   10 (Much Like Me)

. . . .

I feel unsure about myself after I socialize.

0 (Not Like Me)   5 (Somewhat Like Me)   10 (Much Like Me)

. . . .

The HIGHER Much Like Me your score on each of the statements, the more of a socialization problem you have in the insecurity measured. Areas where you scored lower Not Like Me suggest that you are not experiencing too many signs of a gaming problem in that particular aspect. Remember that any scores other than 0 can be indicative of a gaming addiction problem.

All My Friends Are Gamers

Many people with a gaming addiction find it difficult to socialize with people who are not gamers. It can be a viscous circle because it keeps people in the gaming world from socializing with other friends or even relatives. People who are not gamers want to socialize in other ways but gaming. It leaves gamers estranged from loved ones or good friends. However, staying away from them often keeps gamers feeling lonely. Keep in mind, gaming friends may only be your friend if you game. That is NOT a healthy friendship.

Below, identify people in your life who can support you by engaging in something that interests you that has nothing to do with gaming.

Potential People to Help and Support Me USE NAME CODES	Relationship To Me	How This Person Can Support Me
Example: JEY	*JEY is my first cousin and is a great guy.*	*Maybe he can help me find out more about our ancestry. I've been wanting to do that for a very long time.*

Use "I" statements to ask people to be a part of your support system:

"I feel like you really understand me and what I'm going through. I was wondering if you would consider being a part of my social support system?"

"I realize that I have not been very reliable in the past, but I am trying to change some things in my life, and I would like you to be part of my social support system."

"I know I have been difficult to trust lately, but I am getting help, and would appreciate it you didn't give up on me yet. Please be part of my social support system."

Participate Face-to-Face

Many gamers are socially isolated. People addicted to playing video games are often so wrapped up in gaming that they don't realize how many opportunities are available to engage in social activities face-to-face. All it takes is the desire to meet new people face-to-face.

A few opportunities of meeting new people:

- Befriend someone new at work.
- Consider a college class.
- Get a ticket to a sporting event and ask someone to join you.
- Go to the gym and exercise.
- Help others by doing volunteer work.
- Join a club such as a chess club, hiking club, gardening club, reading club, etc.
- Meet neighbors.
- Participate in religious or spiritual activities.
- Take a class in the community (cooking, calligraphy, French, etc.)
- Try out for community arts group such as theater, choir, orchestra, etc.

In the spaces that follow, develop your own list.

Social Opportunities	Why it Appeals to Me	How I Can Get Involved

Build Existing Relationships

You probably know a lot of gaming friends whose relationships tend to be superficial and lack closeness and connection other than gaming. You can fix this by building on existing relationships with people you already know. These people might be family members, friends you have lost due to gaming, co-workers, customers, neighbors, a person you met in the coffee shop, etc.

Identify some of these people and explore ways that you can connect with them again.
(Ask them to go to a movie with you, have dinner get-together, go for a walk together, etc.)

People I Want to Reconnect With (Use Name Codes)	How I Will Go About Reconnecting
Example: GEA	*We used to be friends. After I got into gaming I had no time for her. I will start by telling her that I'm sorry we haven't had time together and I miss being with her. I will invite her out for coffee on Saturday.*

It's fine to have social media that connects us with old friends,
but we need tools that help us discover new people as well.
~ Ethan Zuckerman

Repairing Broken Relationships

Your gaming addiction has probably put a great strain on many of your relationships. Some may be damaged and some may be broken entirely. The good news is that many of your relationships can be healed.

Some of the ways to accomplish this are to ...
- Admit you isolated yourself in order to game.
- Apologize for being unkind.
- Ask forgiveness for harm you may have caused.
- Be humble and describe your flaws.
- Describe how you want to make things right.
- Explain the poor choices you have made.
- Own up to mistakes you have made.
- Take responsibility for your addiction.

How will you repair your broken relationships?
Describe these relationships and how you will attempt to repair them.

Relationship (Use Name Codes)	How I Damaged It	How I Will Repair It
Example: My friend L.L.Y.	We used to go to a movie once a week. Time after time I cancelled at the last minute with a different excuse.	I will be honest and tell him the truth.

Fear of Social Situations

People who are addicted to playing video games often have many fears associated with social situations. It will help you to find ways to decrease your fear of social situations by decreasing your social discomfort. Your inner self-talk is primarily responsible for keeping you fearful. The negative and critical thoughts running through your mind can be harmful in social situations.

Take a look at the typical thoughts in the first column and describe the ones that sound like your inner thoughts in social situations. Then reframe them so they are more positive.

Typical Thoughts	My Specific Thoughts	My Thoughts Reframed
I am boring.	*I am boring and have nothing to talk about except video games.*	*You have many different interests to talk with others about.*
I am boring.		
I know I am weird.		
People usually don't like me when they first meet me.		
People are evaluating and judging me in social situations.		
People will reject me.		
I will be criticized if I make a social mistake.		
I can't take a chance of being socially embarrassed.		
What others think about me defines who I am.		
Why try it if I will only fail?		
Other		

Rebuilding Trust

To re-establish and to maintain effective relationships with people in your life, you need to rebuild trust. Think about the ways you can do this for someone whom you have emotionally or physically harmed because of your addiction to playing video games.

Choose a person in your life who has lost your trust, write about how you can accomplish each of the statements in the boxes below.

A person's name code who has lost trust in me: ___ ___ ___

I will communicate accurate and relevant information by updating information about my current addiction.
I will take responsibility for my mistakes.
I will openly share my thoughts and feelings.
I will communicate with honesty.
I will describe how I will behave better in our relationship.
I will express how I will be trustworthy in the future.

Trust is the most important part of a relationship, closely followed
by communication. I think that if you have those two things, everything
else falls into place - your affection, your emotional connection.
~ Vanessa Lachey

Building Social Skills (Page 1)

SOCIAL SKILLS are the skills we use to communicate and interact with each other, both verbally and non-verbally, through body language, gestures, and personal appearance.

Gaining and/or improving social skills requires practice. People do not become socially competent overnight. They need to put in time and practice to feel comfortable meeting new people, building relationships, and maintaining them. They will not become comfortable in social situations without putting in time and effort. The best way to gain social skills is to start small and take baby steps towards being more confident and social, and then build on those successes.

Following are some of those baby steps you can take.
Try each one, and then journal about how it felt.

If you are in a safe place, smile at people you pass.

How did it feel? _____

_____

How did it feel if someone did not smile back?_____

_____

What thoughts went through your head if someone did not smile back?_____

_____

Compliment others you encounter during your day.

How did it feel? _____

_____

How did it feel if people did not respond? _____

_____

What thoughts went through your head when people did not respond? _____

_____

(Continued on the Next Page)

Building Social Skills (Page 2)

Ask someone an easy question: *(Are the scones good? Do you think it will rain today?)*

How did it feel? _____

_____

How did it feel if the person answered the question? _____

_____

What thoughts went through your head if the person was not nice?_____

_____

Start a conversation with a cashier, co-worker, waiter, or neighbor.

How did it feel? _____

_____

How did it feel if the person was friendly? _____

_____

What thoughts went through your head if the person was not friendly? _____

_____

Join a friendly, social group with people of the same interests. *(choir, book club, etc?.)*

How did it feel? _____

_____

How did it feel to be with people who have interests similar to yours?_____

_____

What thoughts went through your head when talking to these people?_____

_____

I think sometimes in life we want to ignore the problems of society and just think about the good. I believe in positive thinking and affirmative living, I also think it's really important to remember all of our disenfranchised members of society.
~ Kerry Washington

Social Skills

Another important aspect of developing social skills lies in your ability to create, build, and maintain close relationships with friends, neighbors, co-workers, and family.

After each item, circle the number that best describes how well you do using social skills.

Listen attentively by focusing on the present about what others are saying to you, rather than thinking about how you're going to respond, or thinking about gaming.

Not Like Me   1   2   3   4   5   6   7   8   9   10   A Lot Like Me

Pay attention to non-verbal-signs. It is not only about what others say, but how they say it, using body language, eye contact, and tone of voice.

Not Like Me   1   2   3   4   5   6   7   8   9   10   A Lot Like Me

Encourage and support people because we all want to feel heard and respected. When being encouraged they feel more comfortable opening up about how they're feeling.

Not Like Me   1   2   3   4   5   6   7   8   9   10   A Lot Like Me

Be open and honest by expressing true feelings as directly as possible to ensure long- lasting and fulfilling relationships with others.

Not Like Me   1   2   3   4   5   6   7   8   9   10   A Lot Like Me

Show appreciation by paying genuine compliments to the people in your life. When other people feel valued, they're more likely to appreciate and value you.

Not Like Me   1   2   3   4   5   6   7   8   9   10   A Lot Like Me

Make commitments and keep these commitments. Don't over-commit yourself or set unrealistic expectations, but keep commitments to build or rebuild trust.

Not Like Me   1   2   3   4   5   6   7   8   9   10   A Lot Like Me

The higher your score on each of the items, the greater your social skills in that area. Areas in which you scored less than 5 can be increased to help you maintain close relationships.

Tips for Meeting People Offline

It can be difficult for people with a gaming addiction to meet new people offline. They spend so much of their time and energy with video games that they find it difficult to meet new people in their real lives outside of gaming. To meet new people, you need to give your energy, time, and attention, and to show your trustworthiness to other people.

Write about a situation you have avoided because you did not know anyone.

_____

_____

In the situation above, how could you have used the tips below to meet new people. Write your answer on the lines that follow each tip.

Learn as much as you can about a person you have just met, or hardly know. Knowledge is power. The more you know about others, the more you can ask open-ended questions about their lives, and they will admire you for being interested.

_____

_____

Provide information that people request about you. Let others know about who you are outside of the gaming world. *(Family, work, hobbies, volunteering, etc.)*

_____

_____

Ask people open-ended questions about their opinions. *(Example: What did you think about how the movie ended?)*

_____

_____

Be as positive as you possibly can be. If you are sharing something about your gaming addiction or about yourself, be as positive as possible and hopeful for the future. Positive people don't like to be with negative people.

_____

_____

Really listen to what people are saying by staying in the present moment. Don't just seem like you are interested. Focus on what they are talking about, rather than worrying about what they are thinking of you. Don't anticipate what you want to say next. Instead, be present and fully attentive to the feelings behind the content of what others have to say.

_____

_____

Shirking Obligations

Many people who are addicted to gaming harm their social relationships when they shirk important obligations and events to play video games. In your social relationships (family members, partner, children, friends, co-workers, etc.), what obligations have you avoided because you were gaming?

Describe below some of the obligations you have shirked and how that may have affected people close to you (USE NAME CODES).

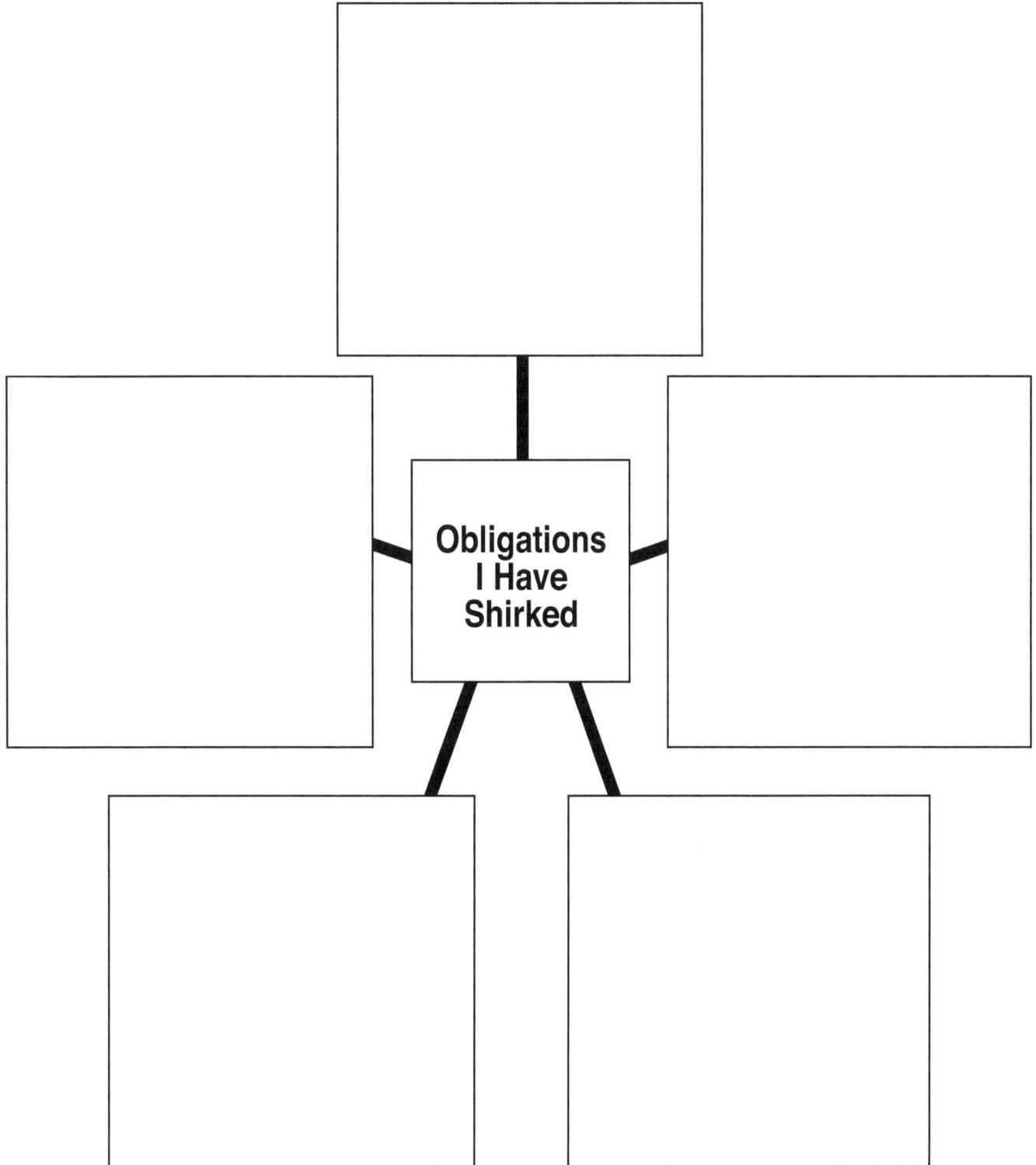

**Obligations
I Have
Shirked**

Relationship Issues – WHY?

Social isolation is often a fact of life for people who are addicted to playing video games. Look at each of the reasons below, place a check mark in front of the ones that apply to you, and answer the question, "WHY?"

I am irritable and people don't want to be around me. WHY? _____
_____

I am not a source of support or encouragement to friends and family. WHY? _____
_____

I am socially awkward. WHY? _____
_____

I can't engage in real-world conversations. WHY? _____
_____

I can't get invested in face-to-face relationships. WHY? _____
_____

I don't enjoy the company of others unless we are gaming. WHY? _____
_____

I do not have the skills to establish friendships and relationships. WHY? _____
_____

I don't have the time or energy for relationships. WHY? _____
_____

I don't know how, when, or where to meet people other than gaming. WHY? _____
_____

I feel left out of conversations. WHY? _____
_____

I feel socially isolated. WHY? _____
_____

I talk about gaming too much. WHY? _____
_____

I lack effective social skills. WHY? _____
_____

Online relationships are easier for me. WHY? _____
_____

People don't want to hang out with me. WHY? _____
_____

Who are some trusted people with whom you can speak about these issues? _____
_____

Quotes about Socialization

*On the lines that follow the quotes, describe which quote(s) speak
to you and your socialization skills.*

I consider social skills a bit like learning a language. I've been practicing it
for so long over so many years I've almost lost my accent.
~ Daniel Tammet

_____

_____

_____

We're building a lifelong relationship with people, and every
great relationship has to be built on trust.
~ Angela Ahrendts

_____

_____

_____

I'm so socially awkward. I really had to put myself out there and meet new people.
~ Bella Hadid

_____

_____

_____

Which quote especially speaks to you and your socialization skills? Why?

_____

_____

_____

_____

_____

Gaming

Self-Control

Name _____

Date _____

Self-Control Assessment
Introduction and Directions

In order to be able to control compulsions, impulses, and urges to play video games, self-control is the key! Self-control is comprised of three distinct traits: willpower, impulse control, and discipline. The following *Self-Control Assessment* was designed to help you explore the ways you are able to control, or not control, your desire to play video games.

This assessment contains 15 statements that measure the three behaviors inherent in being able to display self-control and control of your urges, impulses, and compulsions to game.

Read each of the statements and decide whether or not the statement describes you.
If the statement is TRUE, circle the number next to that item under the "True" column.
If the statement is FALSE, circle the number next to that item under the "FALSE" column.

In the example below, the circled number 2 under "TRUE" indicates the statement is true of the person completing the individual scale.

WILLPOWER SCALE _____ TRUE   FALSE

When it comes to playing video games...
I do not put off what I want in the short term to get
   what I want in the long term. ....(2)...........1

This is not a test.
Be sure to respond to every statement. **Be Honest!**

(Turn to the next page and begin.)

Self-Control Assessment

Name _____ Date _____

Think very hard and be honest in your responses.

WILLPOWER SCALE _____ TRUE   FALSE

When it comes to playing video games...

I do not put off what I want in the short term to get
 what I want in the long term. 2 1

I cannot resist urges to play video games. 2 1

I just cannot control myself when it comes to gaming. 2 1

I am unable to override unwanted thoughts and feelings about playing. 2 1

I make emotional decisions about playing. 2 1

Willpower Scale TOTAL = _____

IMPULSE SCALE _____ TRUE   FALSE

When it comes to playing video games...

I often act or react without thinking. 2 1

I game based on an impulse. 2 1

I don't get the big deal about why it is a problem to game. 2 1

I don't think about the consequences of my behavior. 2 1

I can't seem to control my actions. 2 1

Impulse Scale TOTAL = _____

DISCIPLINE SCALE _____ TRUE   FALSE

When it comes to playing video games...

I cannot control how much I play. 2 1

I have been unsuccessful in reaching my goal to reduce game playing. 2 1

I can no longer manage my impulses to game. 2 1

I feel helpless to change my actions despite the negative consequences. 2 1

I lack persistence in trying to reduce the time I play games. 2 1

Discipline Scale TOTAL = _____

(Go to the Scoring Directions)

Self-Control Assessment

Name (use a name code)_____ Date _____

Scores & Profile Interpretations

The assessment you just completed examines three important behaviors necessary for self-control.

On the previous pages, add the scores you circled and put that number in the line marked TOTAL. Transfer those numbers below by placing each number on the continuum line of the matching Scale below.

Self-Control Assessment Profile Interpretation

Willpower Scale: This scale measures the control you can exert to avoid playing video games or restrain impulses to game.

_____
5 = Low   8 = Moderate   10 = High

Impulse Scale: This scale measures the amount of control you have in regulating your emotions and behaviors that drive you to play video games.

_____
5 = Low   8 = Moderate   10 = High

Discipline Scale: This scale measures the extent to which you can use action or inaction in order to achieve your goal of reducing your addiction to playing video games.

_____
5 = Low   8 = Moderate   10 = High

The higher your score in any of the scales, the less self-control you have in working to overcome your addiction to playing video games and the greater risk you have for experiencing negative effects of a gaming addiction.

However, by circling even ONE Medium or High answer, you can be at risk for experiencing negative effects of excessive gaming on your personal and/or professional life.

Got Grit?

Grit is similar to willpower. It is the motivational drive that keeps you on task over a sustained period of time. It is a mindset that perceives a challenge like your addiction to gaming as an opportunity to learn and grow rather than an obstacle to overcome. You can show grit by responding with constructive thoughts and behaviors that demonstrate persistence rather than defeat.

In the table that follows, describe four times you showed grit and did NOT game.

What Occurred USE NAME CODES	How I Showed Grit	The Result
I was on a winning streak in my game, but SWB asked me to help move furniture.	Even though I was itching to game, I decided that helping a friend was more important.	SWB really appreciated my help and we have become better friends. We hang out a lot and I am gaming less.
1.		
2.		
3.		
4.		

Ways to Enhance Your Level of Grit

- Change your thinking about goals that might seem difficult or overwhelming. Stop negative thoughts such as "I can't do this." or "This is too hard." Challenge these defeatist thoughts and replace them with positive thoughts such as "I have achieved difficult goals before, so these will be easier." or "I have been through tough times much worse than this before."
- Visualize yourself being successful in overcoming your addiction to playing video games. Use your passion for your goals to keep you motivated and picture yourself achieving your goals.
- Remain optimistic no matter what happens. Review your successes so far and remember how you were able to overcome setbacks and mistakes.
- View failure as feedback on how you can be more successful in the future. See mistakes and disappointments as opportunities to do things differently and be successful next time.
- Don't think too big. Focus your attention on achieving your next small goal, and then the next one, and so on. While it's important to keep your overall goals in mind, focus your immediate attention and actions on the next milestone.
- Never give up. Giving up ensures that you will not achieve your goals. Start small and try to take a few small steps to achieve your results. That will give you the energy needed to stay the course, while also building your competence and confidence.

© 2021 WHOLE PERSON ASSOCIATES, 101 WEST 2ND STREET, SUITE 203, DULUTH MN 55802 • 800-247-6789 • WHOLEPERSON.COM

Make it Difficult to Act Impulsively

When you are addicted to playing video games, one of the best methods for reducing the time you spend playing them is to make it more difficult to act impulsively and game. For example, if you tend to play video games in a particular room in your house, ensure that there is no gaming equipment available in that room.

What changes can you make in your environment to make it more difficult to act impulsively?

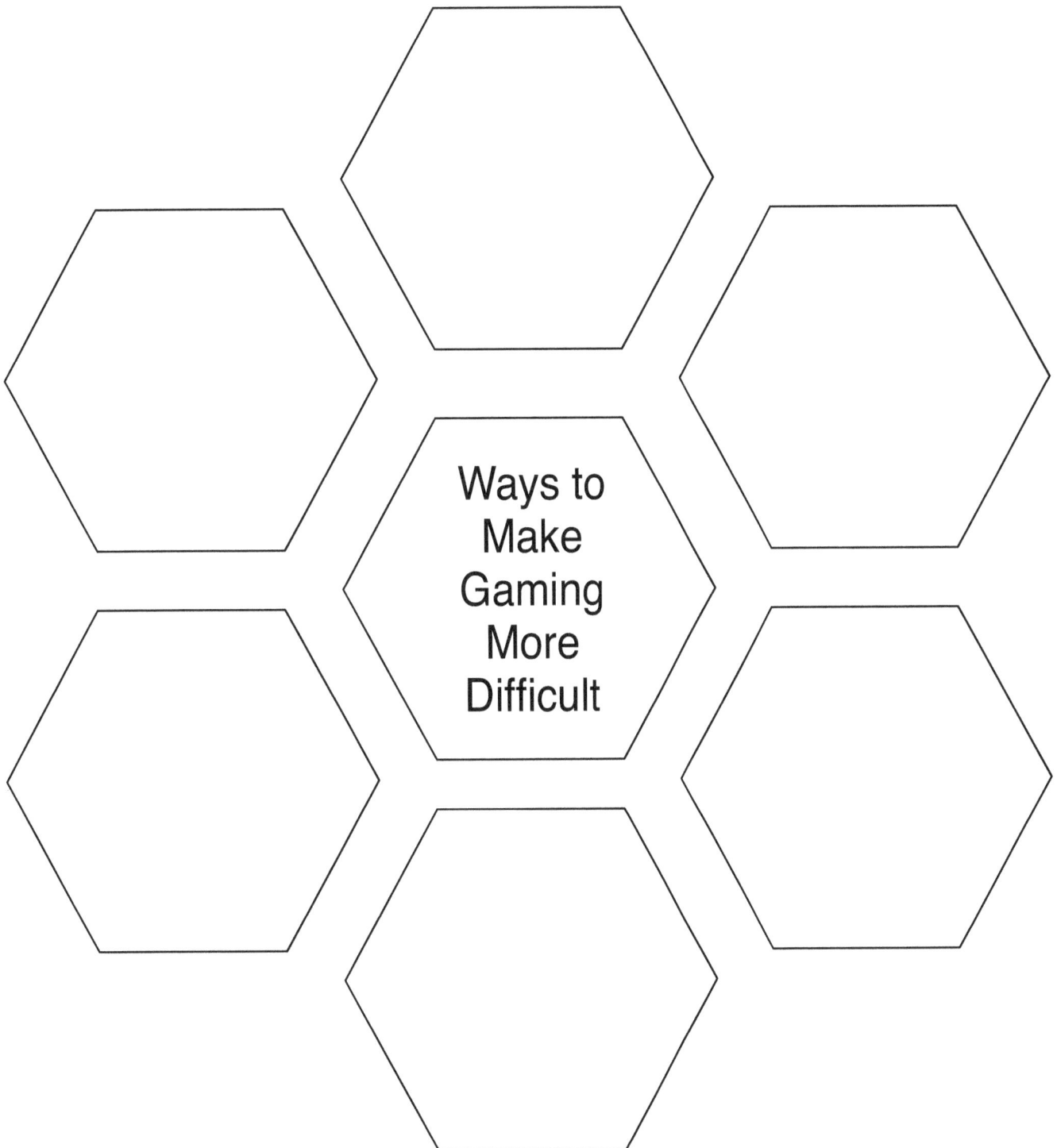

Ways to
Make
Gaming
More
Difficult

What are the Consequences?

People with an addiction to playing video games do not usually think about the consequences of their actions. They will say things like "I'm not hurting anyone." or "I'm not asking you to play!" They often do not notice the long-term consequences that their addictive behavior has on them or on other people. The long-term consequences might be related to a job, health, relationships, finances, etc.

What are the long-term consequences of your addiction to gaming and how can you start thinking more about the consequences of your actions?

Consequences of My Actions	Who It Affects USE NAME CODES	How It Affects Me and Others
Example: Hurting My Relationships	*NKP*	*She has left me. My entire family is angry with me because she won't have anything to do with them because they would not insist that I stop gaming.*

Everybody, soon or late, sits down to a banquet of consequences.
~ Robert Louis Stevenson

What does this quote means to you.

_____

_____

_____

Distract Yourself

When you are receiving impulses to play video games, one method to avoid acting on your impulse is to distract yourself. The first part in distracting yourself entails recognizing the impulsive behavior and distracting yourself when it occurs.

Example: Take a walk, listen to your favorite music, go for a jog, etc. How will you do this when you get impulses to game? USE NAME CODES.

How I Know I am Anxious to Game	How I Could Distract Myself	How This Would Help Me
Example: I start getting antsy and thinking about various games I can play.	*I enjoy keeping fit, so I could exercise at the local gym.*	*I can get into better shape and meet some new people*

You can always find a distraction if you're looking for one.
~ Tom Kite

Do you believe this quote to be true, or not true? Explain.

_____

_____

Time to Calm Yourself

Sometimes impulsive gaming is the result of experiencing unusual amounts of stress or frustration. Relaxing yourself can help to diminish impulsive urges to game.

Try this process, and then describe how it felt and how successful it was.

Focus on Your Breathing. Be quiet for a few minutes, clear your mind and focus on your breathing. When you notice your mind begins to wander toward playing video games, return your attention to your breath. Do this for five minutes and your impulse to game might have diminished.

Add this next step to totally relax and reduce your impulse to play video games.

Progressive Muscle Relaxation. Now that you have started to focus on your breathing, you can quickly deepen the amount of relaxation you experience. Continue to breathe slowly and rhythmically, and then...

- Focus on your toes.
  Relax and let all of the tension go in your toes.
  Feel the muscles going limp, loose, and relaxed.
  Notice how relaxed the muscles feel now.

- Now do the same with your feet, ankles, calves, thighs, and buttocks.

- Feel the relaxation rise up to your stomach and chest.
  Let it stay there for a few seconds.

- Now, feel the relaxation forming in your arms, hands, and fingers.

- See and feel the relaxation stretch up to your shoulders and neck.
  Roll your neck a few times in a clockwise direction to loosen it even further.

- Next, allow the relaxation to reach your head.
  Feel it in your mouth, eyelids, and go to the top of your head.

- Notice how relaxed all of the parts of your body feel.
  Allow any last bits of tension to dissolve.
  Enjoy the relaxation you are experiencing more than you enjoy gaming.

- When you are ready to return to your usual level of alertness and awareness, slowly begin to re-awaken your body.

- This activity should leave you feeling calm and refreshed.

On the lines that follow, journal about how it felt.

_____

_____

_____

_____

_____

An Impulsivity Log

Explore how often you are able or unable to maintain self-control when it comes to gaming. You can do this by keeping an Impulsivity Log of times you were <u>unable</u> to have self-control and times you were <u>able</u> to have self-control.

It is important to document incidents in order to heal. Reproduce this form for multiple weeks.

Days	A Time When You Became Impulsive, and Had NO Self-Control. (Include what you attribute to your loss of self-control.)	A Time When You Became Impulsive, and Had Self-Control. (Include what you attribute to your having self-control.)
Monday		
Tuesday		
Wednesday		
Thursday		
Friday		
Saturday		
Sunday		

Try not to become too upset with yourself when you are unable to show self-control. Simply note it and be conscious of how you will do better next time!

Feelings and Impulsivity

Whether you realize it or not, most of the time there is a distinct connection between your feelings and your desire to game. Think about some of the times you played video games directly after experiencing a strong emotion.

People Involved (Use Name Codes)	The Situation	How This Prompts Me to Want to Game
Example: MPJ	We had a huge argument. I thought he was being unreasonable and he thought the same about me.	To get back at him, I went into a different room and played video games all night. He hates that!

When you are impulsive, what is the connection between your feelings and your addictive gaming behaviors?

_____

_____

_____

© 2021 WHOLE PERSON ASSOCIATES, 101 WEST 2ND STREET, SUITE 203, DULUTH MN 55802 • 800-247-6789 • WHOLEPERSON.COM

Do You Game on Auto-Pilot?

Mindfulness is the act of bringing attention into the present moment and living in that moment without judging yourself and/or others. Many people with an addiction to gaming live most of their lives on auto-pilot and decide to game without even thinking about it.

How often do you game without even thinking? Write about those times below.

Ways I Game on Auto-Pilot	What I Miss Out On	How I Can Be More Mindful
Example: When I come home after work, I automatically start to play my favorite video game.	*I often get so engrossed that I don't even eat dinner with my family.*	*I can be mindful to change my clothes, talk to my family, and eat dinner before I start gaming. Maybe I will get absorbed in the conversations and not game.*

To lead a more mindful life ...
- Find a quiet place away from video games.
- Concentrate on your breathing. Thoughts will pop into your head but do not let them distract you from concentrating on your breathing. Let them pass by.
- Look around. What do you see? What do you hear? What do you smell?
- Pay attention to how you feel while doing this. How do you feel physically? Emotionally?

Thoughts Precede Actions

What we think about often determines how we feel and the actions that we take. Start to explore the thoughts that precede impulsive actions to play video games.

Write about times this week when you had negative thoughts and then acted impulsively to game.

Times I Gamed Impulsively	Thoughts that Preceded My Gaming	How I Could Have Thought More Positively to Avoid Gaming Behavior
Example: Gaming before bed time.	If I play video games, I will not have to think about all of the work I have yet to do tomorrow.	I could have realized that I can easily handle my workload, if I have a good night's sleep.

It takes but one positive thought when given a chance to survive and thrive to overpower an entire army of negative thoughts.
~ Robert H. Schuller

What does this quote have to do with your gaming addiction?

_____

_____

_____

When I Am Least in Control

Think about what happens when you game, or get an impulse or urge to game.

Respond to the questions in the space below. Just write randomly without thinking too much.
USE NAME CODES.

What prompts these urges to game?

_____

_____

Who prompts these urges?

_____

_____

What situations prompt these urges?

_____

_____

When are you least in control of the urges and impulses to play video games?

_____

_____

What is going on in your life when you feel these impulses?

_____

_____

Who is around?

_____

_____

What are you doing?

_____

_____

What are you not doing?

_____

_____

Where are you?

_____

_____

Who do you wish was around?

_____

_____

What are you feeling?

_____

_____

Choose What Your Life is Going to be About

I wanted to write about the moment when your addictions no longer hide the truth from you. When your whole life breaks down. That's the moment when you have to somehow choose what your life is going to be about.
~ Chuck Palahniuk

What does this quote mean to you?

_____
_____
_____

What is meant by "when your addictions no longer hide the truth from you?"

_____
_____
_____

What truths are your addictions hiding about you?

_____
_____
_____

How is your life breaking down because of your addiction to gaming?

_____
_____
_____

Is this the moment when you have to choose what your life is going to be about?

_____
_____
_____

What do you WANT your life to be about?

_____
_____
_____
_____
_____

My Plan of "Getting it Done"

If you hope to achieve self-discipline, you must have a clear vision of accomplishing your goal of being free from your addiction. If you don't know where you're going, you will end up some place else. You need to have a plan of action in order to avoid being sidetracked.

Respond to the following questions to develop your "plan of getting it done." You need to have an understanding of what success means to you.

What will you consider being successful in overcoming your gaming addiction?

_____

_____

_____

How will you know when you are successful?

_____

_____

_____

A clear plan outlines each step you must take to reach your goals. What is your goal?

_____

_____

_____

What steps do you need to take in order to achieve your goal?

Step #1: _____

Step #2: _____

Step #3: _____

Step #4: _____

What are your strengths that will help you reach your goal?

_____

_____

_____

Create a mantra (a positive phrase to say over and over again) to keep yourself focused.
(Example: I can overcome my addiction to gaming)!

MY MANTRA: _____

_____

_____

It's Up to You!

William Johnson said, *"If it's to be, it's up to me."* When it comes to overcoming your addiction to gaming, it is up to you and nobody else. You are responsible for your life and the choices you make.

It is important to make good choices, stop blaming other people, control what you can control, and take the responsibility to control your addiction.

In the spaces below, write about, draw, or doodle your responses.

I will make better choices such as …	I will stop blaming the following people …

I will take control of my life by …	I will take more responsibility by …

© 2021 WHOLE PERSON ASSOCIATES, 101 WEST 2ND STREET, SUITE 203, DULUTH MN 55802 • 800-247-6789 • WHOLEPERSON.COM

The Path of Least Resistance

Many people who are addicted to playing video games often take the path of least resistance, which only deepens their gaming addiction. If one chooses to game when needing to be discussing issues with one's partner, one is taking the path of least resistance. Similarly, if one games when frustrated at work, it would be healthier to talk with your supervisor to resolve the problem than get lost in the fantasy world of gaming. It's time to start living life in the real world rather than the fantasy world.

Below, identify those times you take the path of least resistance and how to stop doing it.

Times I Take the Path of Least Resistance	How to Begin Living in the Real World

The path of least resistance is the path of the loser.
~ H. G. Wells

Substitutions

People addicted to playing video games can benefit from having activities, hobbies, leisure activities, projects, and interests in which to engage instead of video games.

To identify some of your possible substitutions, circle the items below that are of interest to you, and write down some of your own in the space provided.

Arts & Crafts: painting, drawing, sketching, sculpting, photography, writing poems, short stories, music, ceramics, pottery, mosaics, origami, reading, art festivals, community theatre, choir, blogging beading, dancing.

Other: _____

Health & Fitness: tennis, martial arts, yoga, mountain climbing, kayaking, scuba diving, coaching sports, amateur sports, weight lifting, exercising, jogging, aerobics, softball, skiing, bowling, swimming, cycling, outdoor hiking, skateboarding, etc.

Other: _____

Science: astronomy, building model rockets, math puzzles, amateur archeology, meteorology, star gazing, collecting rocks, exploring caves, weather watching, visiting planetariums, prospecting, watching aerospace shows on television, etc.

Other: _____

Social: Volunteering in a hospital, daycare center, library, etc., tutoring, assisting the disabled, working at a homeless shelter, babysitting, caring for children, caring for the elderly, visiting people who are ill, making friends, going to parties or entertaining, going to amusement parks, tutoring; etc.

Other: _____

Home & Family: baking pastries, cake decorating, hosting parties, sewing, cooking, traveling, attending school and athletic activities, watching sports, handling equipment for a local athletic team, serving family meals, canning and preserving food, cooking for community events, etc.

Other: _____

Technology: participate in positive social media responsibly, robotics, programming, building websites, learning HTML, digital scrapbooking, photo editing, repairing computers, computer drawing, animation, blogging, graphic design, etc.

Other: _____

Mechanical: fixing things, woodworking, home repairs, painting, repairing cars, auto body repair, wood carving, metalwork, repairing watches and clocks, furniture repair, upholstery, model railroading, welding, car restoration, metalworking, candle making, leather working, etc.

Other: _____

Plants & Animals: bird watching, riding horses, showing dogs, hiking, nature walks, hunting, fishing, camping, visiting state parks, flower arranging, animal breeding, pet watching, growing house plants, gardening, playing with pets, landscaping, training pets, volunteer at a zoo, etc.

Other: _____

Now think about all of the ways that you can substitute the activities you Identified for playing video games.

Quotes about Self-Control

On the lines that follow each of the quotes,
describe what each quote means to you and how it applies to your life.

Self-control is true power.
~ Marco Pierre White

_____

_____

_____

Sometimes it's good to say no. Sometimes it's good to not act impulsively.
~ Phoebe Robinson

_____

_____

_____

No man is free who is not master of himself.
~ Epictetus

_____

_____

_____

Which quote especially speaks to you about self-control? Why?

_____

_____

_____

_____

_____

_____

_____

Gaming

Healthy Balance

Name _____

Date _____

Healthy Balance Assessment
Introduction and Directions

An addiction to playing video games can change and possibly impair your life. You may find out that many aspects of your life are being affected by your excessive gaming. The *Healthy Balance Assessment* was designed to help you explore how your gaming addiction is changing your life. This assessment contains 30 statements related to various ways your gaming addiction can impair your life.

Read each of the statements and decide whether or not the statement describes you. If the statement is TRUE, circle the number next to that item under the "TRUE" column. If the statement is FALSE, circle the number next to that item under the "FALSE" column.

In the example below, the circled number 2 under "TRUE" indicates the statement is true of the person completing the individual scale.

AGGRESSION SCALE _____	**TRUE**	**FALSE**

My behavior has changed ...

I am becoming more violent...(2).........1

This is not a test. Since there are no right or wrong answers,
do not spend too much time thinking about your answers.
Be sure to respond to every statement. **Be Honest!**

(Turn to the next page and begin.)

Healthy Balance Assessment (Page 1)

Name _____ Date _____

AGGRESSION SCALE _____ **TRUE**   **FALSE**

My behavior has changed ...

I am becoming more violent. 2 1

I am more physically aggressive. 2 1

I become hostile when someone wants me to do something instead of gaming. . . . 2 1

I lack self-control of the time I spend gaming. 2 1

I am expressing hostile emotions more often. 2 1

Aggression Scale TOTAL = _____

WORK/SCHOOL SCALE _____ **TRUE**   **FALSE**

My job/school work has gone downhill ...

I am always tired because I game late at night. 2 1

I am not carrying out my responsibilities as well as I did in the past. 2 1

I liked my projects but I resent them now. It takes time away from gaming. 2 1

I can't concentrate because I am thinking about the next time I'll be gaming. 2 1

I arrive late because I stay up late gaming. 2 1

Work/School Scale TOTAL = _____

HEALTH SCALE _____ **TRUE**   **FALSE**

My health has changed ...

I am having problems with my vision. 2 1

I am gaining/losing a lot of weight. 2 1

I have neck and/or back problems. 2 1

I am developing poor posture from sitting for prolonged periods of time. 2 1

I am experiencing hand / wrist / shoulder problems. 2 1

Health Scale TOTAL = _____

(Continue on the next page.)

Healthy Balance Assessment (Page 2)

FAMILY SCALE _____ TRUE   FALSE

My family life is not what it used to be ...

I have lost the respect of my family members. 2 1

I let my family down. 2 1

I fail to keep promises I make to family members. 2 1

I am aware that my family no longer trusts me. 2 1

I lie to my family to cover up my game playing. 2 1

Family Scale TOTAL = _____

SOCIAL SCALE _____ TRUE   FALSE

My usual social life has gone downhill ...

I no longer want to socialize with friends or family. 2 1

I feel lonely and isolated. 2 1

I lack effective social skills. 2 1

I do not feel comfortable in social situations. 2 1

I have lost personal relationships due to my gaming. 2 1

Social Scale TOTAL = _____

PERSONAL SCALE _____ TRUE   FALSE

My personal life isn't what it used to be ...

I am unable to concentrate like I used to. 2 1

I cannot pay attention to my personal hygiene. 2 1

I am neglecting my hobbies. 2 1

I prefer to live in a fantasy world. 2 1

I find myself making foolish impulsive decisions. 2 1

Personal Scale TOTAL = _____

(Go to the Scoring Directions)

New Lifestyle Assessment

Name (use a name code)_____ Date _____

Scoring Directions & Profile Interpretations

The assessment you just completed looks at the effects of gaming on various aspects of your life.

On the previous pages, total the scores you circled and put that total in the box marked TOTAL. Then, transfer that number below. Place each number on the continuum line of the matching Scale below.

Assessment Profile Interpretation

In each of the sections, place an X on the line to note your score.

Aggression Scale: This scale measures the extent to which gaming is making you more aggressive and violent.

5 = Low	**8 = Moderate**	**10 = High**

Work Scale: This scale measures the extent to which gaming has affected your job performance.

5 = Low	**8 = Moderate**	**10 = High**

Health Scale: This scale measures the extent to which gaming has affected your physical health.

5 = Low	**8 = Moderate**	**10 = High**

Family Scale: This scale measures the extent to which gaming has affected your family life.

5 = Low	**8 = Moderate**	**10 = High**

Social Scale: This scale measures the extent to which gaming has affected your social life.

5 = Low	**8 = Moderate**	**10 = High**

Personal Scale: This scale measures the extent to which gaming has affected your personal life.

5 = Low	**8 = Moderate**	**10 = High**

The higher your score in any of the scales, the greater risk you have for experiencing negative effects of gaming. However, by circling even ONE medium or high response, you can be at risk for experiencing devastating effects on your personal and/or professional life.

My Level of Functioning

A gaming addiction can cause a lack of functioning in all areas of one's life. Often, people experience a level of life impairment as a result of a gaming problem.

Below, identify how you are functioning and your level of impairment. You can respond in both columns or just one of them. Look at the three examples provided.

Areas of My Life	My Level of Functioning	My Level of Impairment
Example: Aggression		*I want to confront people who are against me like I do in my video games.*
Example: Aggression	*I am working on calming exercises to use when I get aggressive with others.*	
Example: Aggression	*I am trying to be gentle with my family because I love them so much.*	*Even though I hear them, I usually can't stop my anger when they want me to stop.*
Aggression		
Work		
Health		
Family		
Social		
Personal		
Other		

Focus on being balanced - success is balance.
~ Laila Ali

© 2021 WHOLE PERSON ASSOCIATES, 101 WEST 2ND STREET, SUITE 203, DULUTH MN 55802 • 800-247-6789 • WHOLEPERSON.COM

Better Life Balance

When people have a healthy balanced life, they pay attention to all aspects of themselves and their life. They do not focus solely on one area of their existence. They attend to the many aspects of their lives.

Below explore how much time a day you are spending with the many aspects of your life. Your total time should add up to 100 %.

Time	Percentage
24 hours	100%
20 hours	83.3%
16 hours	66.6%
12 hours	50%
8 hours	33.3%
4 hours	16.7%
0 hours	0%

Aspects of My Life	Percent of Time I Spend Each 24-Hour Day	In the Future I Would Like to Spend this % Each Day
Emotional and/or Caring for others		
Family Time		
Finances		
Gaming		
Physical/Exercise		
Relationships		
Religious/Spiritual		
Sleep		
Work Time		
Other _____		
Other _____		
Other _____		

It is important to find ways to balance playing video games and the other aspects of your life. Take control of your life. Choose what you want to do and then plan the percentage of time you want to spend doing it.

Readily Available Environments

One of the reasons that gaming has become so popular, and so problematic, is that it is so readily available. Changes in your various environments will allow you to develop a routine and create positive, healthy habits so that you do not have to rely on conscious willpower.

What are some of the changes you can make?

Environments	How Gaming is Available	How I Can Make it Less Accessible
Example: Home	*Gaming stuff in every room.*	*Have a designated gaming room with limited gaming hours.*
Example: Work	*Video games on my work computer.*	*Take them off before I get fired.*
Home		
Work		
Educational Facility		
Sports Venue		
Concert / Movie		
Shopping Mall		
Restaurant		
Community Center		
Place of Worship		
Other		

Ways to "Game-Proof" your environments:
1. Set time limits for play and stick to them.
2. Engage in plenty of non-game activities.
3. Keep phones and other gadgets out of the bedroom so you won't play into the night.
4. Do self-care every day, including exercise.
5. Remember the motto: When games are out of sight, they are also out of mind.

© 2021 WHOLE PERSON ASSOCIATES, 101 WEST 2ND STREET, SUITE 203, DULUTH MN 55802 • 800-247-6789 • WHOLEPERSON.COM

My Current Routine

Most people have busy lives, and many different priorities. It is important for everyone, especially people with a gaming addiction, to develop a routine schedule. Gaming can be a part of your life if it is reasonably scheduled and the schedule is followed. This activity will allow you to take a look at your priorities and to ensure you are not excessively gaming.

In each segment, list the activities you are engaged in on a typical gaming day in your life. Circle the day that you game the most. BE HONEST!

My Current Routine on: SUNDAY, MONDAY, TUESDAY, WEDNESDAY, THURSDAY, FRIDAY, SATURDAY

Morning	
Afternoon	
Evening	

How much time did you spending that day playing video games? _____

My Ideal Routine

Most people have busy lives and many different priorities. It is important for everyone, especially people with a gaming addiction, to develop an ideal routine schedule for their time. Remember that gaming can be a part of your life as long as it is reasonably scheduled and the schedule is followed. This activity will allow you to take a look at your priorities and ensure you are not excessively gaming.

For each segment of a typical day, list the activity in which you would ideally be engaged.

My Ideal Routine – A Typical Day

Morning	
Afternoon	
Evening	

How much time did you spending that day playing video games? _____

Develop Coping Skills

People who are battling a gaming addiction need a wide variety of coping skills. These coping skills can be cognitive, physical, emotional, and spiritual.

In the spaces that follow, identify some of the coping skills you use when you want to game. For each coping skill, identify whether you use it or not, and the effect it has on you.

Coping Skills	Used (U)/Not Used (N)	Effect of The Coping Skill
Attend a meeting		
Call a friend for support		
Cook or bake		
Do a project with a friend or co-worker		
Exercise or do something physical		
Go to the park		
Help someone		
Indulge in a creative activity		
Listen to music		
Meditate		
Take a warm shower or hot bath		
Take several slow, deep breaths		
Turn negative thoughts to positive ones		
Volunteer		
Write about your feelings in a journal		
Other		

Gaming Addiction Time Frame

It is important to explore the developmental course of your gaming addiction. An addiction to playing video games usually begins as a great hobby that over time becomes a problem. It will be helpful for you to begin tracking exactly how your gaming behavior came about and the effects it has on you and on your life. Journal your responses to the questions posed below:

My age at when I started gaming _____ **My age now** _____

Gaining and/or improving social skills requires practice. People do not become socially competent overnight. They need to put in time and practice to feel comfortable in meeting new people, building relationships, and maintaining them. They will not become comfortable in social situations without putting in time and effort. The best way to gain social skills is to start small and take baby steps towards being more confident and social, and then build on those successes. _____

_____

This is what was occurring in my life when I became addicted _____

_____

The reason(s) that I started gaming _____

_____

This is how gaming affects me emotionally _____

_____

This is how gaming affects me physically _____

_____

This is how gaming affects my family/my close relationships _____

_____

This is how gaming affects me in a positive way _____

_____

This is how gaming affects me in a negative way _____

_____

This is what occurs when I try to stop gaming _____

_____

This is what I can do about it _____

_____

_____

© 2021 WHOLE PERSON ASSOCIATES, 101 WEST 2ND STREET, SUITE 203, DULUTH MN 55802 • 800-247-6789 • WHOLEPERSON.COM

My Serenity Prayer

The Serenity Prayer is regularly recited in addiction programs written
by the American theologian Reinhold Niebuhr (1892–1971).

Niebuhr used various versions of the prayer widely in sermons as early as 1934. The prayer spread rapidly, often without attribution to Niebuhr, through church groups in the 1930s and 1940s and was adopted and popularized by Alcoholics Anonymous and other twelve-step programs. The Serenity Prayer appeared in a sermon of Niebuhr's as part of the 1944 *A Book of Prayers and Services for the Armed Forces,* while Niebuhr himself first published it in 1951 in a magazine column.

> *Grant me the serenity to accept the things I cannot change,*
> *The courage to change the things I can,*
> *And the wisdom to know the difference.*

In the space that follows, rewrite the serenity prayer to better fit you, your personality, and your issues. You may make it longer, shorter, or change it in any way you want.

Example:
Grant me the inner peace and grit to accept what I cannot change,
The courage and perseverance to change the way I am living my life,
The ability to reduce the time I am spending playing video games,
And the wisdom to make better choices.

Now write your own Serenity Prayer

Grant me _____

_____

_____

_____

_____

_____

_____

_____

_____

_____

_____

_____

If you wish, share your version of The Serenity Prayer with others.

Gaming Consequences

People who experience joy and wellness in life are able to take a long-term look at their behavior and explore which behaviors are adding meaning and joy to life for the long-term, as well as those that are not adding meaning and joy to life for the long-term.

Dig deep and think about the long-term consequences of your gaming addiction and write them in the lower boxes under Personal, Occupational, and Relationship Well-Being.

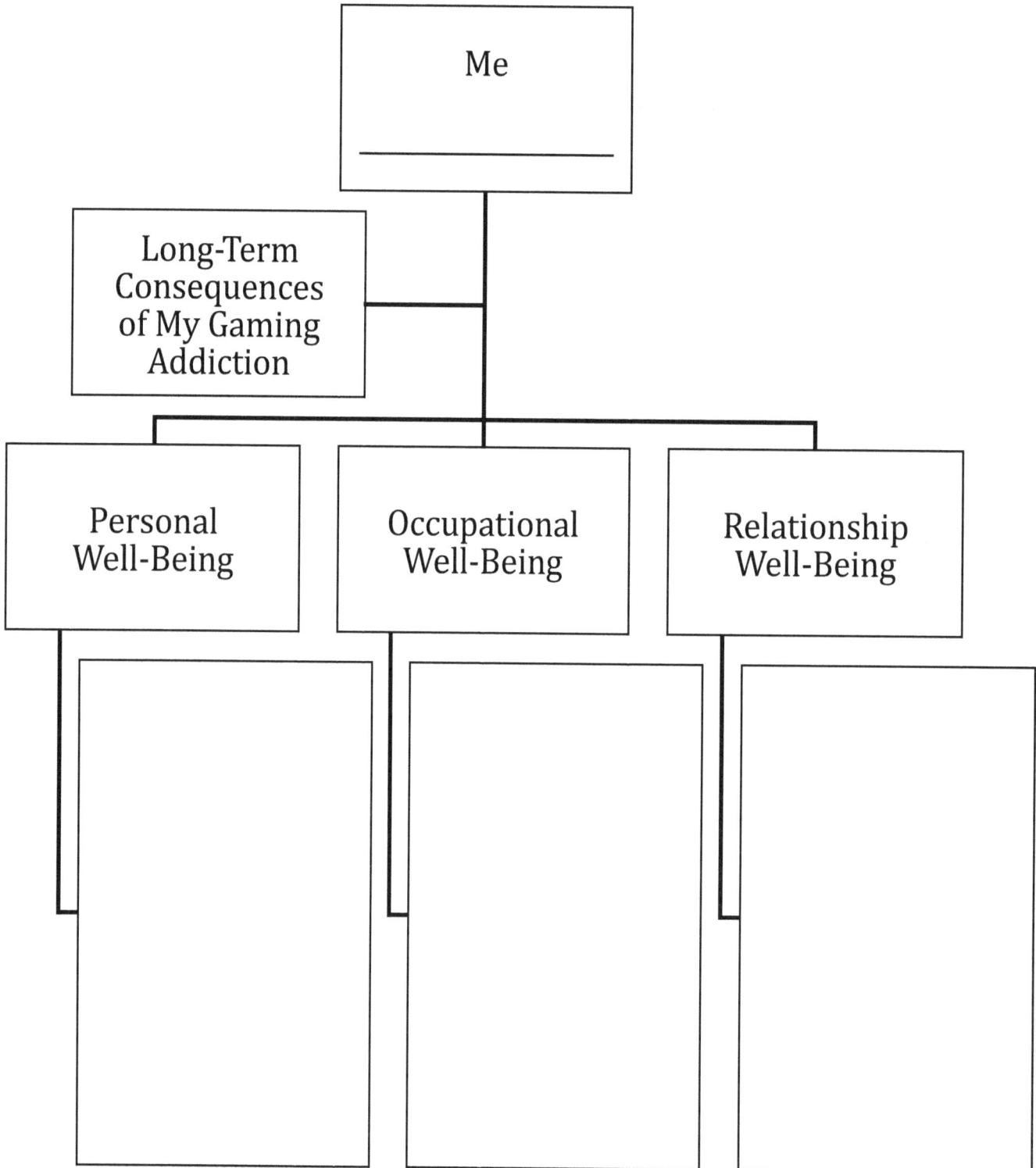

Me

_____

Long-Term Consequences of My Gaming Addiction

Personal Well-Being

Occupational Well-Being

Relationship Well-Being

Healthy Choices

People who are addicted to anything usually make poor choices. They might choose to skip work, even if they have a presentation to make, in order to engage in their addiction.

Think about some of the poor choices you have made pertaining to gaming and write about them below. Then describe how you can begin to make healthier choices.

Healthy Balance	My Typical Poor Choices	My Healthier Choices
NUTRITION: *Are you eating 3 healthy meals a day and avoiding quick-fix junk foods?*		
RELATIONSHIPS: *Are you spending quality time with the important people in your life?*		
SLEEP: *Are you sticking to a bedtime routine that is not changed because of gaming?*		
PLEASANT ACTIVITIES: *Are you enjoying non-gaming activities that bring you joy?*		
EXERCISE: *Are you spending time outdoors, doing physical activities, and exercising?*		
GAMING: *Are you aware of the amount of time you spend gaming each day?*		
Other		

In which area(s) of your life are you making healthy choices? _____
_____

What are the ways you can make even healthier choices? _____
_____

In which area(s) of your life are you NOT making healthy choices? _____
_____

What are the ways you can make healthy choices in the areas above? _____
_____

Healthy Distractions

Here is a healthy strategy: When you have an urge to play video games, think about some of the ways that you can use healthy distractions to curb the urge. (These distractions DO NOT include such activities as drinking alcohol, drug use, eating binges, risky activities, etc.)

Identify some of the healthy distractions you can use when have the urge to play your favorite video game after gaming for hours.

Example: cognitive activities such as playing chess or doing a math puzzle on paper; creative activities like singing or drawing; and physical activities like taking your dog for a walk or feeding and/or watching birds.

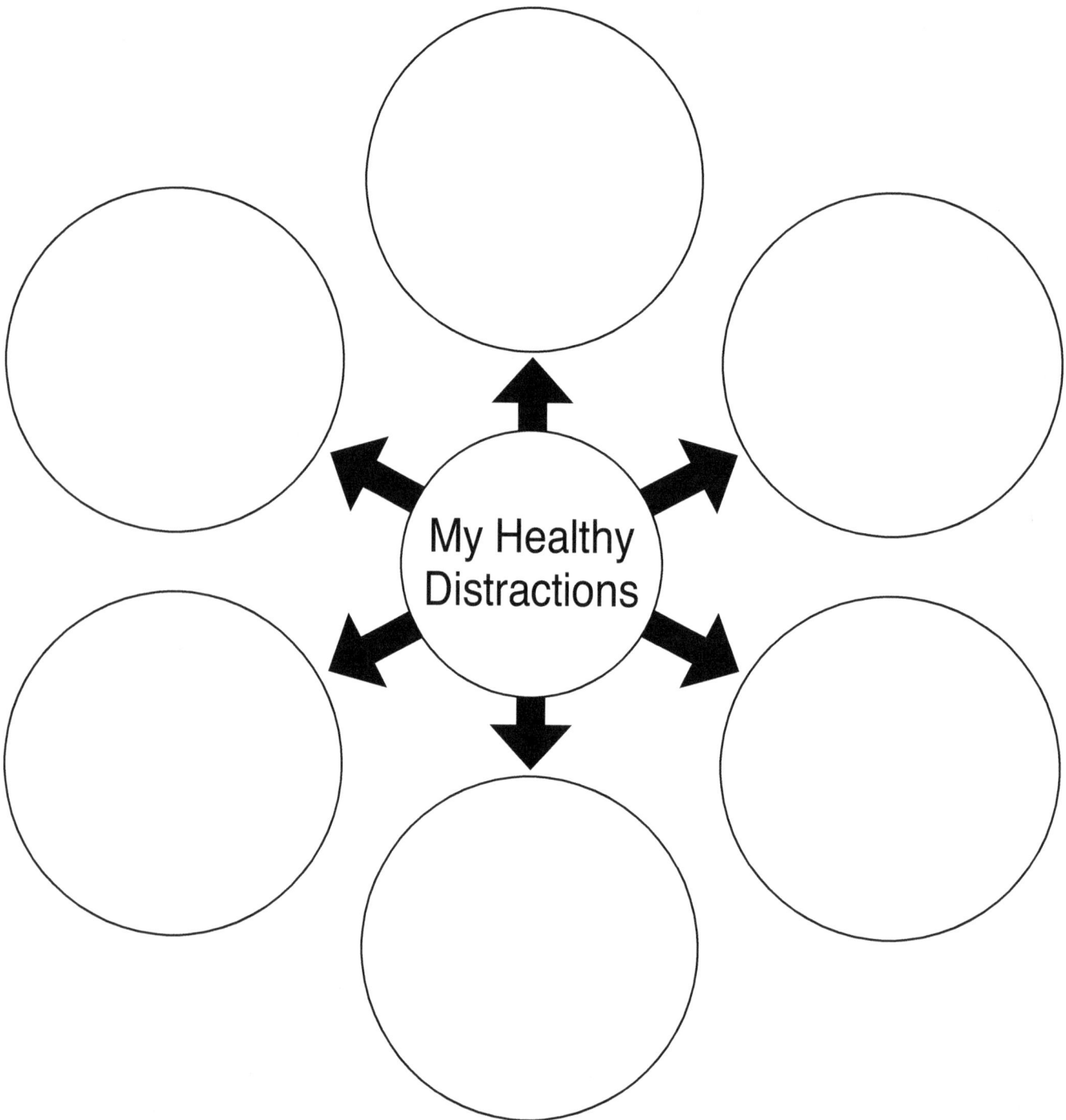

My Healthy Distractions

Neglecting Yourself

People who play video games in excess and then realize that they are addicted to gaming, often find that they are neglecting themselves. Estimate how many hours per week you play video games and then respond to the boxes below. (Be honest, no one needs to see this)

I play video games about _____ hours per week!

Write, draw, or doodle your responses below to describe how you are neglecting yourself.

1. Neglecting My Responsibilities: *For example, I am putting gaming first and then getting up late for my obligations, letting people down, not following through on promises, etc.*	**2. Neglecting My Appearance:** *For example, I am forgetting to shower, I am wearing the same clothes every day, not washing or combing my hair, brushing my teeth, and neglecting all of my personal hygiene.*
3. Neglecting My Health: *For example, I am not sleeping well, not eating properly, feeling anxious, gaining or losing weight, have physical problems, not taking time to go to a doctor, and feeling generally unhealthy.*	**4. Neglecting My Finances:** *For example, I'm spending too much money on games and accessories, not working enough, not paying my bills or paying the people to whom I owe money, and not saving any money.*

What is one thing you will do to rectify the situations in each of the areas above?

1. _____

2. _____

3. _____

4. _____

Exploring My Losses

People with a gaming addiction often have many losses: relationships, a job, an educational opportunity, spirituality, money, self-control, pride, ability to have a good night sleep, etc. What have you lost because of your addiction to gaming?

My Losses	The Consequences	My Response to These Losses
Example: I lost my job	*I am in financial trouble, I have no references for another job, and my family is furious with me.*	*I have started looking for a new job, but I can't find one, and it takes time away from my gaming.*

I can choose to sit in perpetual sadness, immobilized by the gravity of my loss, or I can choose to rise from the pain and treasure the most precious gift I have - life itself.
~Walter Anderson

Everyone has difficult times in life. It is how they respond to these difficult times that define their character, quality of life, and the opportunity to reevaluate the time spent with gaming.

How will you respond to your losses?

_____

_____

_____

A No-Gaming Contract

Complete the following **No-Gaming Contract** to help you develop a plan for reducing the amount of time you spend with video games.

Sign and date it, put it on your refrigerator or bathroom mirror, and look at it every morning.

I, _____ will do whatever it takes to stop playing video games excessively. My addiction to gaming is causing the following problems in my life ... _____

_____

_____

_____

_____.

To win the war against excessive gaming, I am willing to make the following overall changes to live a healthier, more joyful, life:

1. _____

2. _____

3. _____

4. _____

5. _____

In addition, I will avoid playing video games and spend more time engaged in the healthy behaviors I have listed below *(examples: meditating, enjoying time with my family, re-acquainting with friends, etc.):*

_____

_____

_____

_____   _____

NAME   **DATE**

Quotes about a Healthy Balance

On the lines that follow each of the four quotes, describe how the quote speaks to you and your desire for a healthy life balance.

Everybody, soon or late, sits down to a banquet of consequences.
~ **Robert Louis Stevenson**

_____

_____

_____

Resilience isn't a single skill. It's a variety of skills and coping mechanisms.
To bounce back from bumps in the road as well as failures, you
should focus on emphasizing the positive.
~ **Jean Chatzky**

_____

_____

_____

I think that it's just about balance, keeping myself centered, and being happy and healthy.
~ **Normani Kordei**

_____

_____

_____

Goal setting should be part of your daily and weekly routines and
should not be based on a calendar year or month.
~ **Lewis Howes**

_____

_____

_____

Which quote especially speaks to you and your future goals and plans? Why?

_____

_____

_____

© 2021 WHOLE PERSON ASSOCIATES, 101 WEST 2ND STREET, SUITE 203, DULUTH MN 55802 • 800-247-6789 • WHOLEPERSON.COM

WholePerson

Whole Person Associates is the leading publisher of training
resources for professionals who empower people to create and
maintain healthy lifestyles. Our creative resources will help
you work effectively with your clients in the areas
of stress management, wellness promotion,
mental health, and life skills.

Please visit us at our web site: **WholePerson.com**.
You can check out our entire line of products, place an order,
request our print catalog, and sign up for our monthly
special notifications.

Whole Person Associates
800-247-6789
Books@WholePerson.com

www.ingramcontent.com/pod-product-compliance
Lightning Source LLC
Chambersburg PA
CBHW082358270326
41935CB00013B/1676